The Country Life Guide to

Horses and Ponies of the World

The Country Life Guide to
Horses and Ponies
of the World
Elwyn Hartley Edwards
Illustrated by David Nockels

Country Life

COUNTRY · LIFE
NEWNES·BOOKS

Published by Country Life Books
an imprint of Newnes Books, a Division
of The Hamlyn Publishing Group Ltd

First published 1979
Second impression 1984

ISBN 0 600 34533 5 (softback)
ISBN 0 600 34492 4 (cased)

Printed in Spain by Printer Industria Gráfica, S.A.   Barcelona
Depósito Legal B. 39217-1983

Contents

Introduction

The earliest known ancestors of the horse inhabited the earth about sixty million years ago, when man was not identifiable as a species. But it was only four thousand years ago that the Indo-European tribes living on the steppes north of the Black and Caspian seas first began to domesticate the descendants of the earliest horses. Until then, and for many years after, the horse population developed in accordance with the dictates of environment and natural selection. Environment still plays a part in the modern, domestic horse, even though it is often an environment controlled by humans, but except in the case of wild or half-wild horses (and there are not many of those in the twentieth century), reproduction by natural selection has now been replaced by breeding programmes planned by man. This human intervention is the most decisive element in equine development and is largely responsible for the varieties and breeds which make up the horse population of the world today. When man first appreciated the advantages of horse-power he used the raw material which he found under his hand; later, he shaped it in numerous forms to suit his purposes and needs, striving for his own ideal of perfection.

In that respect modern horses are the product of human application. But it would be impossible to ignore the importance of the millions of years of natural selection which provided the basic stock for improvement. Today, Arabian horses are bred all over the world in areas that in no way resemble the desert lands which were the home of their forbears. Similarly, Welsh ponies are bred in places where conditions of climate and terrain are vastly different, and far from, their native hills and moorlands. But in both these examples it is the qualities and character imposed by the original environment that breeders seek to retain. The evolution of a type of horse or pony with special, inherent characteristics is the result of its environment and the process is a very long one. Certainly, it is beyond the capacity of one man in his lifetime or even of a hundred men in theirs, for humans, unlike nature, do not have the centuries at their disposal. Breeders can only improve upon the products of environment up to a certain point. If they are unwise enough, in their attempts to produce bigger or more refined specimens, to go beyond that point, they run the risk of losing qualities that have been fixed by nature over hundreds and thousands of years. When that situation is reached the stock begins to degenerate.

Breeds and types of horses and ponies do exist that are almost 'man-made' even though they must as with all living things be based on old-established stock. An example is the unique British Riding Pony, possibly the world's nearest approximation to equine perfection. The Riding Pony is not yet established as a breed; its origin is too recent for that. It is, in fact, an amalgam of native blood, mostly

Welsh, Thoroughbred, and Arab. In order to preserve its pony character together with the attributes of bone, substance and an acceptable degree of hardiness, endurance and stamina, resort must still be made from time to time to the reinvigorating native stock from which the Riding Pony came. That is the importance of environmental influence and it remains a vital factor in breeding. The people of the very earliest times recognized its importance, as do the world's surviving pastoral tribes today. Among such peoples it was, and in some parts of the world still is, the practice to loose in-season donkeys, mares or cows to mate with wild males of the same species and thus reinvigorate the domestic stock. A study of the breeds described in this book shows that their continued existence and viability depends on retaining the qualities and characteristics formed by the environmental background of the base stock. It can be argued that the Thoroughbred, the aristocrat of the horse world and a breed that has had an enormous influence in the improvement of so many other breeds, is, in fact, an 'artificial' product since, although the breed is directly descended from the Arabian horse, no modern racehorse has Arab blood close-up in its pedigree. The modern Thoroughbred is, indeed, a remarkable achievement; it is far larger, infinitely more elegant and incomparably faster than the early product. However it is neither as sound nor enduring as the 'prototype' racehorse, which was more closely related to the Arab. No present-day horse could compete in stamina with a horse of the calibre of The Great Eclipse (1764–1789), who often ran three four-mile heats in a day, under weights that would now be unthinkable, and was never beaten. For the moment the future of the Thoroughbred is secure, but within the next century it could become necessary to reintroduce an element of Arabian blood to prevent the racing stock from degenerating.

At this point, since the word has been mentioned frequently, it is appropriate to attempt a definition of 'breed'. In modern conditions and, therefore, allowing for human intervention, a breed, to qualify for that title, is composed of a group of horses or ponies which have been selectively bred for a sufficient length of time to ensure the consistent production of stock which has clearly defined common characteristics of height, colour, conformational appearance and action. Such stock is the offspring of 'pure-bred' parents with pedigrees recorded by the breed's governing body in a breed Stud Book. They, in their turn, are also eligible for similar registration.

As an example we have only to turn again to the Arab and the Welsh Pony. Both are bred universally but are immediately recognizable by unmistakable features and characteristics which are faithfully reproduced from one generation to the next.

Horses and ponies of these two distinctive breeds are all registered in Stud Books and it is possible to trace their breeding back over many generations.

In both these cases, as with many other established breeds, the improving hand of man is evident, but it is possible for a breed to exist as such without human interference and without benefit of Stud Book. The Arab and the Welsh Pony were clearly definable types long before there was any idea of selective breeding other than by natural means, and thousands of years before anyone thought of keeping breeding records. (In fact, Stud Books are a fairly recent innovation; many are not more than a hundred years old, and some even less than that.) The last of the existing 'primitive' horses, the Tarpan and the Asiatic Wild Horse, which descend respectively from the prehistoric Plateau and Steppe Horses, were clearly established and uniform many thousands of years ago and the present day 'primitives' are much the same as they ever were.

If it was possible in our fast-shrinking world to find a group of ponies in some inaccessible part hitherto unknown to men, where the herd had been isolated from centuries of outside influences, a new breed would have been discovered. No records would be available but in other respects the group would fulfil all the criteria necessary to be accorded the status of a breed. Their characteristics of size, appearance and so on would have been fixed by the environment in which they existed, and to which they would have adapted by natural selection.

The environmental factors affecting the type of animal produced include soil conditions, feed availability and climate. Mountain-bred ponies are small in stature since they have to subsist on a meagre diet and endure harsh weather conditions. They are highly efficient converters of food, they grow heavy coats as a protection against winter winds, rain, snow and ice and they also develop other qualities which aid their struggle for survival. They are naturally tough and hardy, their feet have dense horn to withstand the effects of the rocky ground and they acquire an action best suited to crossing the broken terrain in which they live. The surefooted mountain pony bends the knee to prevent himself falling over rocks and tussocks, and develops a healthy respect for boggy ground.

In the same way horses bred in desert conditions are adapted to their environment, although the resulting animal is quite different to the mountain-bred horse. Horses bred in ideal conditions with plentiful feed, equable climate, and a limestone sub-soil grow much larger and do not need to acquire an action like that of the mountain pony, or the ability to withstand extremes of heat and drought like the desert-bred horse. On the other hand they are less hardy and do not develop the initiative found in horses bred in harsher conditions.

The factors which influenced men in their improvement of horse types were more variable. Initially the early horse peoples regarded their horse herds as convenient larders of fresh meat on the hoof and as a source of milk. Hides were used to make clothing and shelter and horse dung provided easily-gathered fuel. The idea of using horses as pack and draught animals came later. Firstly the horse was used as a pack animal. Then came the earliest form of

Fig. 1 Stages in the evolution of the horse
(a) Eohippus (b) Mesohippus (c) Merychippus (d) Pliohippus

draught hauling, a *travois.* This was an arrangement of two poles, one fastened to each side of the horse, with the ends trailing on the ground behind. The space between the ends, when joined together, provided a platform for the load. Almost three thousand years later the North American Indians used a similar device.

The invention of wheeled transport greatly influenced the development of the horse. In warfare, early cavalry formations were carried in horse-drawn chariots rather than on horseback. This led to an emphasis on the rearing of large, fast harness horses with good endurance. To achieve this, chariot horses were often hand-fed.

The first evidence we have of a ridden horse is a relief on the tomb of Horenhab of Egypt, dating from about 1400 B.C. Later mounted warriors replaced charioteers and once more the emphasis changed, this time to the improvement of suitable riding horses. At the same time the movement of armies, bringing them into contact with the people of other lands and with their horses, resulted in many cross-breedings. Increasing agricultural productivity made fodder more plentiful and helped to produce bigger and better horses.

In Medieval Europe heavy horses capable of carrying armoured knights and hauling heavy loads were in demand. When knights became obsolete, because of the immobility imposed by their heavy armour and their vulnerability to firearms, the heavy horse, altering in form to suit new demands, continued to play an essential part in agriculture and transport. Until the nineteenth century, when steam-power and later the internal combustion engine began to displace horse-power, the economy of the world largely depended on horses. They were integral to all forms of overland transport, and to agriculture and warfare, as well as being a means of sport and recreation. They were therefore to be found in every shape and form, adapted to many different purposes. There were heavy and light draught horses, carriage horses, trap ponies, cavalry remounts, pack and riding animals, hunters, cobs and ponies – all forming our vast equine heritage.

Today, the role of horses is largely confined to sport and recreation and their use as work animals is in decline. The old heavy breeds have diminished in numbers because there is little demand for them. The international trend is towards producing competitive saddle horses – racehorses, show jumpers, event horses, dressage performers – and, of course, to breeding more and more ponies for children to ride.

Today's equine heritage, with its proliferation and variety, is the result of 4,000 years of development since horses were first domesticated – a short space of time in the evolutionary time-scale of the horse.

Sixty million years ago when our ancestors were no more than 'unidentifiable lemuroids', the earliest form of horse, as far as we know, lived on the earth and is believed to be the ancestor of the modern wild and domestic animals. Scientists, who discovered amazingly complete remains in North America only a century ago, called it Eohippus, the Dawn Horse, or less lyrically, *Hyracotherium,* suggesting a relationship with the rodents.

In fact this first ancestor so little resembled the modern horse that the discoverers of this skeleton did not immediately associate it with the equine species at all. Eohippus, from the reconstruction the scientists were able to make from the bones, was no larger than a fox, standing only about thirty cms high. The forefeet were equipped with four toes, while the hind had three.

From this discovery it could be shown fairly conclusively that the equine species originated in what is now the North American continent. Some million years ago a recognizable horse had evolved there, much smaller than its modern counterpart but a horse for all that, and by that time had migrated into South America, Asia and Europe. Later, after the disappearance of the Bering land bridge, horses became extinct in the Western Hemisphere. Why they should have done can only now be a matter for conjecture – there is no supportable explanation. (The cradle of the equine species was therefore left empty of horses until the arrival of Christopher Columbus at the island of Hispaniola, now Haiti, in the year 1490 A.D. Columbus took with him thirty horses and by the time of his death in 1506 the Spanish had established breeding centres on the islands of the West Indies. Thirteen years later, when Cortez landed in Mexico with eleven stallions and five mares, the horse was finally reinstated on the continent in which the species had evolved.)

Over many millennia Eohippus was superseded by Mesohippus, a larger, three-toed browsing animal. Mesohippus, in turn, gave way in the Miocene period (about twenty-five million years ago) to Merychippus, which was again larger and more closely resembled the horse as we know it. The teeth were better adapted and although the feet were still three-toed the animal seems to have used only the central ones. The first single-hooved animal, Pliohippus, evolved in the Pliocene period (about seven million years ago) and was three or four times the size of Eohippus, just about 12 hh.

This animal was the forerunner of *Equus caballus,* the modern horse. By the time the human race was becoming established horses had reached the height of about 13 hh. Our horses of today, in all their variety, descend from just three prehistoric types which developed in areas distinctive in terrain and climate. These 'basic horses' are called the Steppe, the Forest and the Plateau horses. (A fourth, the Tundra horse of the Northern Hemisphere, seems to have had no discernible effect upon present-day species. It is interesting to note, though, that remains found in the Yana Valley may indicate that one strain of the little known Yakut pony owes its origin to the lost white Tundra type.)

The Steppe Horse survived almost unchanged, probably because of its inaccessible habitat, as the Asiatic Wild Horse of Mongolia (*Equus Przewalskii Przewalskii Poliakov*), which was discovered on the Mongolian steppes by Colonel N. M. Przewalskii in 1881. On the western edges of the Gobi desert, where it was first found, this primitive horse has now been hunted to near extinction, but it is preserved in several zoos.

The Forest horse was a much heavier, slower-moving animal with large feet suited to the swampy, forest conditions in which it lived. It was the basis for the 'cold-blood' heavy horse breeds of Europe which still exist in large numbers today. The Plateau type was a much finer horse than the Forest type, and was lightly built. It had long, slender limbs and its feet avoided the narrowness and extreme length of the Steppe hoof and the broad large feet of the Forest Horse. Today, the Plateau horse is represented by the Tarpan, a breed which is still preserved in Poland. Whether the Tarpan is more than a close replica of the original wild Tarpan is a matter for conjecture, since the last truly wild survivor was reported to have been killed near Askania Nova in Russia nearly a century ago. The present herds were collected from peasant farms in the nineteenth century and put into reserves by the Polish government. It seems, however, that the present Tarpan cannot be much different in its essentials to the original Plateau horse. The modern assumption is that the light horses and ponies which constitute today's 'warm-blood' population are descended from the Tarpan.

Here then are the beginnings of the modern breeds described in this book. However it is wrong to assume that all horses belong to a specific breed. Certainly they may be related to one or more breeds but a large proportion are the product of crosses and not pure-bred, many of the unknown and certainly unrecorded and of no fixed character and apperance. These are termed 'types', not breeds, and some of them are very notable. Principal among the horse 'types' are the following:

Hunter

While this book is not intended to pay greater attention to the horses of any one country in preference to those of others, the hunter tends to be associated with Britain and very particularly with Ireland. (This is the case, too, with riding ponies, cobs and hacks, all of which are less typical of other countries.)

Essentially a hunter is simply a horse used for hunting, and may be of any size or shape. However, when one discusses hunters and hunter types one has a clear mental picture of a particular kind of horse: the sort that will carry a rider safely, comfortably and rapidly across country without risk of strain, and will do so once or twice a week throughout a hunting season. Such a horse, particularly if it carries a fair percentage of Thoroughbred blood may also, if it has the temperament for the game, be suitable for high class jumping and eventing. Most hunters of this quality are half-bred, that is, a cross between a Thoroughbred and possibly a good roomy mare possessed of bone and substance but of no known breeding. Others may be as much as seven-eighths bred or even, occasionally, Thoroughbred, in which case they belong to a breed and not a type.

Quite a lot of hunters have native blood in their backgrounds and those that have can be very good indeed – clever, sensible horses that will creep an awkward fence or fly a straightforward one. Some, and they are just as good, will have a little 'cart' blood. A straight cross between Thoroughbred and one of the bigger native breeds, like the Highland, can also produce an excellent horse which is short-legged, active and up to weight.

Traditionally, however, Ireland is the great source of hunter breeding and many of that country's horses go all over the world as jumpers and eventers. The Irish hunter has acquired a great reputation by virtue of performance in the field, which is probably the result of the early handling it receives. Young horses in Ireland benefit greatly from being led and long-reined over the formidable banks of that country, thereafter being ridden over these obstacles in a snaffle bit and usually on a long rein. In consequence they quickly become able jumpers and learn to look after themselves. Even the largest horses are as clever as cats over a big country. A further advantage enjoyed by the Irish horse is that of an equable climate combined with the famous limestone pastures which give bone, substance and size to young stock.

In the past the Irish hunter was frequently bred out of an Irish Draught mare by a Thoroughbred. But the Irish Draught is not now as numerous, although great efforts are being made to maintain and increase its numbers. The Irish Draught is by no means beautiful but almost without exception these horses have strength, excellent limbs and bone and good steady dispositions. When crossed with a Thoroughbred the result is a big, galloping horse, up to weight, temperate yet bold, and balanced and versatile because of its early training.

Hack

A hack is regarded as a 'type' although many are pure Thoroughbreds. An almost equal number have Arab blood as well and some can be part-bred Arabs or even straight Anglo-Arabs. In the past these essentially British products were of two types, the covert hack and the park hack. The former was used to carry its master to the meet in some style but usually at a fairly strong canter, while the hunters were being ridden quietly. The park hack, which is the show hack of the present day, was still more refined and elegant, even less suited to the hurly-burly of the hunt than the covert hack, but ideal for riding in the park in the company of a lady before the appraising eye of the public. The park hack had to be a beautiful horse with great presence; substance and bone measurement were of little account but it had to have perfect manners while moving with great gaiety and freedom. This remains the objective of the modern show hack, whose role is now confined to the ring.

Cob

Although other countries have cobs these utility animals are something of a tradition in Britain. Cobs are strong, stocky animals, big in body with powerful, short legs and rarely standing above 15.3 hh. Their heads are usually large but should show quality. Originally cobs were dual-purpose animals going as well in harness as under saddle. They are generally regarded as 'confidential' horses, steady and sensible and ideal for heavy elderly riders who want a comfortable ride and still enjoy a day with hounds. The cob is, however, by no means a slug and can usually gallop and jump with the best.

Many good cobs were, and to an extent still are, bred in Ireland out of Irish Draught mares put to polo pony stallions, but all sorts of combinations, sometimes unlikely ones, will produce these useful animals.

Riding Pony

During the last thirty years or so a race of riding ponies has evolved in Britain which is unique. Usually between 13.2 and 14.2 hh., these superb little animals are in fact 'mongrels', but very aristocratic ones, and they change hands at very big prices. All ponies bred today are really 'riding ponies', particularly the smaller native breeds, but the 'British Riding Pony' is exceptional and deserves special mention. The base of the pony is usually Welsh but this type has acquired in the course of its improvement both a dash of Arab and a sprinkle of Thoroughbred.

Riding Ponies are very numerous in Britain but there is also a trend towards a pony of more substance, the Working Hunter Pony, which is becoming increasingly popular.

Polo Pony

Present day polo ponies are not, in fact, ponies at all – all are well over 15 hh. since the height limit was removed earlier this century. Nor are they regarded as a 'breed'. The great majority are Thoroughbred and most of them are Argentine-bred. Therefore they do not resemble the English Thoroughbred race-horse very much, having a typical wiry quality of their own. Not all polo ponies are pure-bred; many Indian ponies have Waler blood in their pedigrees. Any active horse can play polo, but with the exception of those Asian countries where 'true' ponies are used, there is a very definite type exemplified by the ponies of Argentina, a country that specializes in their production and seems to be able to produce ponies with an almost in-bred talent for the game.

The breeds that are described in the remainder of this book are listed under their country of origin, with the exception of the Arab and Thoroughbred which are given pride of place. Readers will, however, appreciate that breeds of horses overlap political frontiers which, particularly in Europe, have been subject to constant change. For these reasons breeds may be found in countries other than that of their origin.

The descriptions of the various breeds is for the most part the result of my own observations, and where observation has not been possible I have had recourse to the study of pictures and the descriptions given by authorities on this fascinating subject. Occasionally I have reinforced these summaries of conformation, appearance and so on with the descriptions given by the breed societies. In some cases, however, I have found these to be more a matter of wishful thinking than of fact and so have expressed a personal opinion.

In this respect, while I have made every effort to be objective, I must point out that my eye for a horse is conditioned largely and naturally by the specimens which I see daily in my own country. I am well aware that my view of equine perfection may not always coincide with that of observers in other countries, and with that excuse I apologize for any unintentional offence that may have been given.

The Universal Breeds

The Arab and its direct derivative, the Thoroughbred, originated in Arabia and England respectively. Both these breeds, the most influential in the development of the modern equine are, however, bred and used in almost every horse country of the world, the largest population of both being in the United States. Because of their importance and to prevent unnecessary repetition they are given pride of place at the beginning of this guide.

Arab Horse

Appearance Entirely distinctive. A supremely refined horse of great beauty. Gay in action and carrying head and tail high, the latter like a banner. The head is notable for its outstanding beauty. The face is dished, the forehead broad, eyes very large and prominent, muzzle small with large, flared nostrils, ears small and alert. The coat and the mane and tail are remarkably silky in texture.
Height 14–15 hh (average).
Colour Chestnut, bay, grey, occasionally black.
Temperament and Characteristics Courageous and fiery but very gentle. Great powers of stamina and endurance; very sound and able to carry weight out of proportion to its size.
Uses An all-round riding horse with particular talent for endurance riding. Arabians, the most prepotent of all breeds, are used extensively as crosses with every type of horse and pony for the purposes of upgrading.
Origin Arabia, but now bred throughout the world. This is the oldest and purest of breeds, and a recognizable Arab type is depicted on Egyptian relics dated at *circa* 2000 B.C. The Arab historian, El Kelbi (A.D. 786), traced the pedigrees of Arabians to the time of Baz, great-great-grandson of Noah who, it is said, captured and tamed the wild horses of the Yemen.

Thoroughbred

Appearance Aristocratic and refined. Exceptionally well proportioned. Fine head on a graceful neck running into clearly defined withers and a long, sloping shoulder. Deep girth, strong back and powerful quarters. Limbs strong and with good bone measurement 20 centimetres (8 inches) below the knee. There are slight variations in type between, for instance, the compact sprinter and the bigger-framed steeplechaser.
Height Average 16·1–16·2 hh but specimens below and above average can be seen.
Colour Brown, bay, grey, chestnut, black.
Temperament and characteristics Highly courageous, sensitive and sometimes nervous. The fastest horse in the world and the ultimate in riding horses.
Uses Primarily racing. Used as a cross to produce all types of saddle horses.
Origin England, but bred all over the world. Descended from Arabian horses imported in the 1600s and 1700s and crossed with native running mares. The three founding fathers of the Thoroughbred are accepted as being the Byerley Turk, imported in 1689; the Godolphin Arabian, which came to England from France in 1728; and the Darley Arabian, brought to England in 1705. These horses were responsible for the Herod, the Matchem, and Eclipse lines respectively. Many of the world's breeds have benefited from Thoroughbred outcrosses.

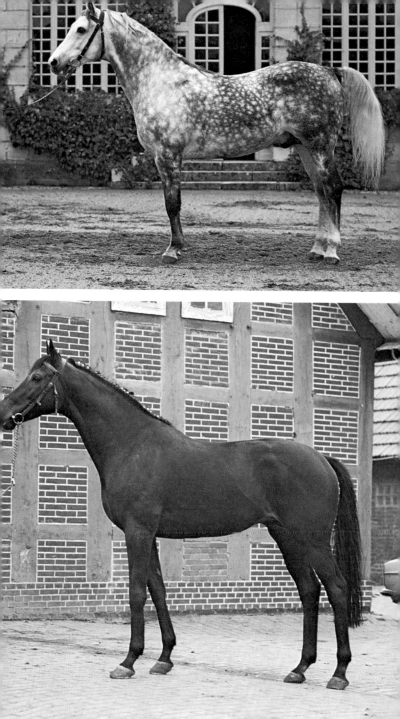

Horses and Ponies of the World

Great Britain

Cleveland Bay

Appearance A handsome, strongly built horse. Large, convex head, long neck, good shoulder. Exceptional depth to the girth. A very strong, slightly long back. Good quarters, well-set tail. Short, strong legs with ample bone. Good feet.

Height 16—16·2 hh.

Colour Bay.

Temperament and characteristics Intelligent and sensible. Very strong and enduring, excellent constitution. Long lived, very fertile. A natural jumper.

Uses A riding and carriage horse capable of farm work, but much valued as a cross with Thoroughbred to produce middleweight hunters, showjumpers, and speedy carriage horses.

Origin North-east Yorkshire, England. A very old breed established for well over 200 years. It was once a packhorse and known as the Chapman Horse. It is probable that there were infusions of Andalucian in its early history and certainly there was a Thoroughbred influence towards the end of the 1700s, otherwise there are no known outside influences.

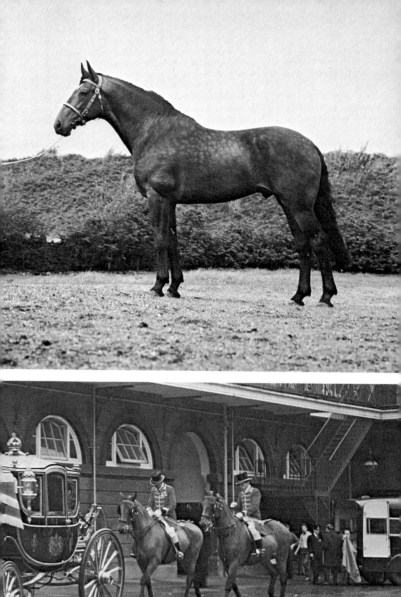

Clydesdale

Appearance A powerful draught animal having exceptional feet and active movement. Short backed with long quarters and almost cow hocks but with very muscular thighs. Straight shanks with much feather.

Height About 16·2 hh.

Colour Bay, brown, roan and black with a lot of white on face and legs, and sometimes on the body.

Temperament and characteristics A kindly horse and very active. Much attention has been given to the feet of the Clydesdale and to developing the perfection of the lower limbs in respect of the action. In consequence, both have exceptional wearing qualities.

Uses Heavy draught, but particularly in urban conditions necessitating road work.

Origin Lanarkshire, Scotland. The breed originates in the Clyde valley and early stock was drawn from Flanders and Denmark in the reign of Edward I. In the late 1700s the native stock was reinforced by the use of Flanders stallions to produce the modern Clydesdale and meet the urban transport needs of the Industrial Revolution.

Dales Pony

Appearance A heavy horse in miniature, complete with feathers on the legs but showing more quality and the refinement of a pony head. Great bone, blue-black feet.

Height 14–14·2 hh.

Colour Black, dark brown; occasionally grey.

Temperament and characteristics Sensible and docile. Hardy, very strong and, up to big weights, sure footed and good, free movers.

Uses A reliable trekking pony and a good performer in harness. Formerly used as a pack pony and for all farm work. A good cross with Thoroughbred to produce foundation stock from which hunters and other types can be bred.

Origin Eastern side of the Pennines, England. The Dales, with the larger variety of Highland, is the heaviest of the British native breeds. It can carry a 100-kilogram (16 stone) man or pull a tonne load. The ponies have been bred in the northern dales for generations and must have something in common with their neighbours, the Fells. There is evidence of some outcrossing and 100 years ago the Welsh Cob, Comet, competing in local trotting matches, was used on Dales mares. All modern Dales trace back to this horse.

Dartmoor

Appearance A refined, graceful pony. Small, intelligent head with little prick ears. Good, sloping shoulder of real riding type. Hard, well-formed legs and good feet.

Height Up to 12·2 hh.

Colour Bay, black, brown.

Temperament and characteristics Sensible and very kindly with children. Very sure footed. The good shoulder and well-held head and neck give a feeling of great security to small riders.

Uses An ideal, trustworthy child's pony which is also valuable as a foundation for the breeding of larger riding ponies.

Origin Dartmoor area of Devon, England. Ponies have inhabited this area from ancient times but until the end of the 1800s the type varied considerably. In 1899, a section for the Dartmoors was opened in the Polo Pony Society's Stud Book (now the National Pony Society) and a breed standard introduced. Outcrosses of Arab blood are certainly present but there is an important Welsh outcross also through the stallion, Punchinello, which was used on Dartmoor in the early part of the century.

Exmoor

Appearance A stronger type of pony than the neighbouring Dartmoor. Deep chested with a short, thick neck. Broad forehead with thick, short ears. A unique characteristic is the hooded 'toad' eye and the coat, which is virtually of double texture. In winter, it is thick, harsh, and springy; in summer it grows close and hard and has a distinctive metallic shine. The tail, an 'ice' tail, is thick with a fan-like growth at the top.

Height 12·2–12·3 hh.

Colour Bay, brown, and a distinctive mouse dun with a mealy muzzle. The mealy effect extends to the underbelly and between the thighs. No white markings.

Temperament and characteristics Independent and sometimes wilful if not correctly handled. Capable of carrying very heavy weights, exceptionally tough and hardy in every way and most enduring.

Uses A tough young person's hunting pony if properly broken but more valuable as a foundation stock for breeding bigger horses.

Origin Exmoor area of Devon and Somerset, England. Once more the early origins are lost in the early days of history. It is possible that the Exmoor was descended from the original Celtic pony and there is considerable evidence for this assumption. The formation of the Exmoor jaw is different to that of any other breed and markedly similar to that of prehistoric ponies. The present-day ponies on the Moor are now reduced to three principal herds. Small numbers of Exmoors are bred away from the Moor but there is a tendency for them to lose type and it is necessary to return to the moor-bred pony to re-invigorate stock.

Fell

Appearance To the uninitiated a smaller, lighter edition of the Dales Pony with a better riding shoulder.

Height 13–14 hh.

Colour Black, dark brown, bay and occasionally grey.

Temperament and characteristics Sensible, hardy and strong. Good head carriage due to the slope of the shoulder. Sure footed and free moving.

Uses A good riding and hunting pony which goes just as well in harness. An excellent foundation for hunter breeding but, as is frequently the case with the larger pony breeds, the best mating is a pony stallion to a Thoroughbred mare.

Origin Northern edge of the Pennines and the Lake District, England. Descended from the indigenous ponies bred on the fells and extensively used for all sorts of farm and pack work, and for the local sport of trotting. There is a theory that these ponies may have been influenced by the Friesian Horse crossed with the now-extinct Galloways of the west Scottish lowlands. In which case, the same would, in part, be true of the Dales with which the Fell must share some common ancestry.

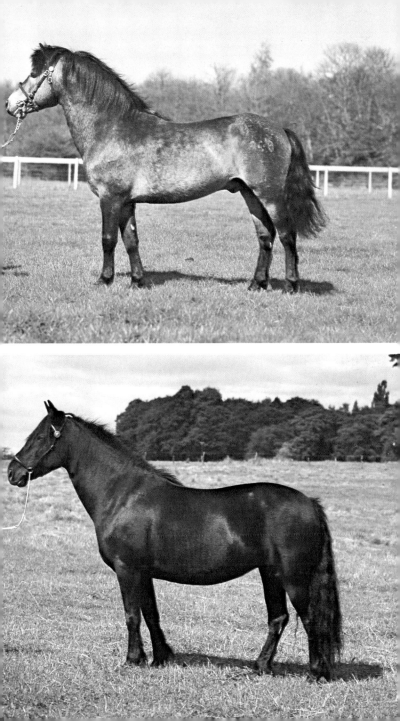

Hackney Horse and Pony

Appearance A spectacular horse. The head is straight and the face convex. The head held high on a curved, muscular neck. Withers rather thicker than in the riding horse but shoulder laid well back.

Height Horses, 15–16 hh; ponies 12·2–14·2 hh.

Colour Bay, brown, black, or chestnut, often with white markings.

Temperament and characteristics Fiery and courageous, and with a spectacular elevated trot in which each foot is momentarily suspended. A brilliant action with enormous thrust from the hind legs. A horse of great presence and personality.

Uses Show-ring harness work. Occasionally used in coach teams.

Origin England. The modern Hackney came into being about the same time as the Thoroughbred, being the product of native trotting mares put to Oriental stallions. The Norfolk Trotter, later known as the Norfolk Roadster, was well established in the 1700s and had been much improved by the foundation sire, Shales the Original, a son of the Thoroughbred, Blaze, by Flying Childers, a hallowed name in the General Stud Book. The Hackney Pony, treated as a separate breed by the Hackney Horse Society, owes much to the Hackney Horse but descends from the old Wilson trotting ponies of Westmorland (Cumbria). Most English Hackneys are now descended from Matthias (1895) through his son, Buckley Courage, and his grandsons, Mersey Searchlight and Solitude.

Highland

Appearance A big, large-bodied pony giving an impression of strength rather than speed. Strong legs with fine, silky hair at the fetlocks. Hard, round feet. The Western Isles type is more refined and smaller.

Height 12·3–14·2 hh.

Colour Varying shades of dun from mouse to gold, and deep, bloodstone chestnut, with flaxen mane and tail, black, bay, and grey. Almost all have pronounced dorsal stripes.

Temperament and characteristics Sensitive and intelligent, if initially wary, but steady. Sure footed, very strong and up to weight.

Uses General farm work, driving, trekking and more ambitious riding. Highlands are still used to carry down deer shot on the hills. A good cross with Thoroughbred blood to produce hunters.

Origin Scotland and the Western Isles. The breed is very old, possibly descended from the North European Horse. Cave drawings at Lascaux, France, estimated as being 50 000 years old, show horses very similar to the Highland in colouring and conformation and with the barred, 'zebra' legs which often occur in the modern pony. To the outside observer, the breed comprises two distinct types, the bigger Mainland Pony and the lighter, more active Western Isles Pony which is of riding type. Much foreign blood is present in the Highland. The Western Isles Pony had a strong infusion of Arab, and earlier the Mainland had been improved by French breeds sent to James IV of Scotland by Louis XII of France.

New Forest

Appearance A pony of good substance and scope. Shortish neck with fairly large head. Good legs with short cannons and hard feet. There is still, however, a variation in type.

Height 12·2–14·2 hh.

Colour Any except piebald or skewbald.

Temperament and characteristics Intelligent and friendly. Hardy. A very good riding pony for children or adults and usually traffic-proof because of its environment in the New Forest area where it comes into daily contact with all sorts of vehicles on the intersecting roads.

Uses An all-round riding pony particularly suited as a family mount and an ideal hunting pony.

Origin New Forest area of Hampshire, England. There have been ponies in the Forest for over 1000 years so that it would be impossible to trace the Forester's origin with any certainty. From the earliest times, the Forest was on the thoroughfare to Winchester, once the English capital, and to the west. The opportunities for the crossing of domestic stock, of all types, with the wild ponies was, therefore, limitless. In more recent times, from the 1800s onwards, a variety of breeds was used to improve the Forest stock including Arab, Thoroughbred, Welsh, Dartmoor, Exmoor, Highland, and Fell. Marske, the reputed sire of the great Eclipse, covered New Forest mares for a period of four years from 1765. Not surprisingly, there is much variation in type and size among the ponies still running in the Forest. Type has, however, become much more fixed in the products of private studs devoted to the breed. The modern ponies running in the Forest are without a doubt as tough, hardy, and as well able to subsist on poor fare, as any other native breed, but among them is a fairly high percentage of scrub stock. Nonetheless, this 'wild' stock, with its inherent pony qualities, is the foundation for the more refined Forester bred by private individuals and now in great demand on the Continent.

Shetland

Appearance A powerful, deep-bodied, miniature pony, standing on short, well-made limbs with small, hard feet. Abundant mane and tail, and very thick coated in winter.

Height Up to 101 centimetres (42 inches) at the wither; average is about 97 centimetres (38 inches).

Colour Any, including part-colours, the most common being black and dark brown.

Temperament and characteristics Independent and intelligent. In proportion to its size, this tough little pony is probably the strongest of its species. Treated as a pony, not as a teddy bear, the Shetland learns quickly and is friendly and docile.

Uses Originally used for work on the crofts of its native habitat. In the 1800s the Shetland was also bred for work in the mines. Today, it is bought as a pet, as a riding pony for very small children and has achieved notable success as a harness pony.

Origin Shetland and Orkney Isles. The earliest trace of the Shetland Ponies is in the remains of those domestic ponies of the Bronze Age (2500 years ago) found on the islands. Possibly the Shetlands are descendants of the Tundra Ponies which came to Britain before the withdrawal of the ice fields and then, over the course of centuries, became reduced in size as a result of their environment (the Tundra Ponies were bigger animals, about 13·2 hh). When Shetlands were in demand as pit ponies, the head was frequently large and heavy. This has been refined in the modern Shetland and the pony is remarkably popular throughout the world, particularly on the Continent where France, Belgium, the Netherlands, Sweden, and Denmark all have their own stud books for the breed. In general, the breed does not accept outcrosses successfully, but attempts have been made. The American Shetland, a harness pony, is the result of a cross with Hackney Ponies, although it can today hardly be said to resemble the pure Shetland. The breed is also at the base of the Pony of the Americas, a Shetland stallion having been bred to an Appaloosa mare, and it was also instrumental in the production of the pygmy pony, the Falabella.

Shire

Appearance A massive, powerful horse, probably as large as any in the world. A big-barrelled horse of great strength with a fine head in proportion to its size. Long legs with abundant feather.

Height 17–18 hh.

Colour Bay and brown, black and grey. Dark colours are always accompanied by white markings.

Temperament and characteristics Sweet-natured, gentle horse, easily managed for all its great size and weight. Shires may weigh over one tonne and have immense strength, being capable of drawing exceptionally heavy loads. A good Shire can move five tonnes while a pair, yoked tandem, have been known to move 18·5 tonnes.

Uses Heavy draught. A farm worker as well as a horse for urban transport.

Origin The Shire counties of the English midlands. The Shire is the descendant of the medieval Great Horse and was founded on the Old English Black. In recent years there has been a great revival of interest in the heavy breeds and particularly in the Shire. In Britain there are still Shires working the land and hauling brewer's drays in the city streets. Ploughing matches are popular and numerous and the well-filled Shire classes at shows, both in-hand and driven classes, are always sure to attract crowds.

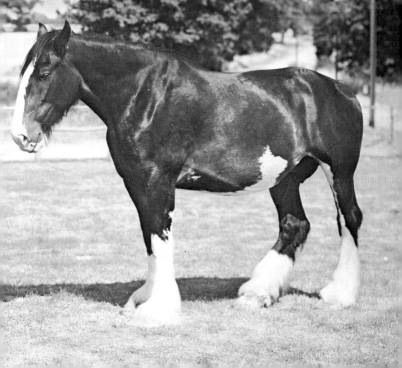

Suffolk Punch

Appearance A compact, big-bodied, horse standing on short, clean legs.
Height 16–16·2 hh.
Colour Chestnut of seven shades ranging from bright to dark.
Temperament and characteristics A genuine worker with a gentle disposition. The breed is very long lived and Suffolks are economical feeders.
Uses Heavy draught. Farm and urban transport worker.
Origin East Anglia, England. The breed is old and remarkably pure. It dates back to 1506 but modern Suffolks all derive from one horse, Crisp's Horse of Offord, foaled in 1760. This very active breed, weighing about one tonne, is retained largely by enthusiasts for showing purposes but some still work on farms and at drawing brewer's drays.

Welsh Mountain Pony (Section A)

(The Welsh Stud Book includes all the Welsh breeds dividing them into Sections A, B, C and D.)

Appearance A very beautiful pony with a lovely head. The face is dished, the muzzle small, and the eye, the glory of the breed, large and luminous. Small prick ears and an alert, intelligent gaze. The pony is exceptionally well proportioned with the deep-girthed body set on limbs of bone and substance. The feet are hard and blue-black.
Height Up to 12 hh.
Colour Any except part-colours.
Temperament and characteristics Courageous with a distinctive Celtic 'fire' but gentle and very intelligent. Excellent, quick, free movement with some bending at the knee, as befits a mountain pony, and going with pronounced engagement of the hocks. Tough, enduring and with an excellent constitution.
Uses A superb child's riding pony and just as good in harness. The breed has equal value as foundation stock for the production of bigger ponies and horses. There is a high percentage of Welsh blood in all of the crossbred riding ponies.
Origin The ponies have been indigenous to the Welsh mountains and moorlands since time immemorial. Julius Caesar founded a stud at Bala, Merionethshire (Gwynedd) and introduced some form of Eastern blood. Nineteenth-century crosses included the Arab and the Thoroughbred, through the stallion Merlin and others, and there is also some evidence of the use of Norfolk Roadster blood. Otherwise the Welsh Pony has remained free from outside influence for very many years and is the most popular as well as the most numerous of the pony breeds.

Welsh Pony (Section B)

Appearance A bigger pony than the Mountain and of more pronounced riding type. Full of quality.
Height Up to 13·2 hh.
Colour As with the Welsh Mountain.
Temperament and characteristics Courageous but gentle and intelligent. The Welsh Pony retains the qualities of the Mountain Pony from which it descends but has more scope and a longer, lower action.
Uses A top-class riding pony.
Origin Wales. The Welsh Pony, derived from the Mountain and the smaller Welsh Cob (Section C) with an admixture of Thoroughbred blood, was once used extensively for shepherding. It is now acknowledged as the finest type of purebred riding pony.

Welsh Cob (Section C)

Appearance A larger edition of the Mountain Pony, bigger built and usually without quite so much refinement in the head.

Height Up to 13·2 hh.

Colour As with the Welsh Mountain.

Temperament and characteristics Kind, steady, and courageous and, in common with the other Welsh breeds, easily kept and constitutionally sound. Pronounced free-trotting action. A good jumper.

Uses Once the general-purpose farm pony, the smaller of the Welsh Cobs is still a great harness pony as well as being in much demand for trekking. The Section C is also an excellent child's hunter and the ideal transition mount between pony and horse.

Origin Wales. The Welsh Cobs have been traditional in Wales for centuries. They derive from the Welsh Mountain, certainly, but in time long past there is some evidence of Andalucian influence and after that the influence of the old Welsh carthorse of Pembrokeshire (Dyfed). More recently (about 100 years ago) there have been infusions of Norfolk Roadster blood and then that of the Hackney. The smaller Cobs flourished in the areas of Brecon and Radnorshire (Powys) and were used for shepherding, hunting, and harness work. The bigger Cobs (Section D in the Welsh Stud Book) belong firmly to Cardiganshire.

Welsh Cob (Section D)

Appearance Larger than the Section C but ideally following the conformation of the Mountain Pony.

Height 14·2–15·2 hh.

Colour Predominantly bay, black, brown, chestnut, roan.

Temperament and characteristics Fiery and courageous, with great powers of endurance and famed for their ability as trotters.

Uses As a harness horse, a pursuit in which the breed excels, and also as a riding horse. The Welsh Cob is a first-rate hunter in all but a galloping grass country and a very good jumper. An excellent cross with the Thoroughbred to produce short-legged hunters of stamina.

Origin Wales. The Welsh Cob (Section D) is associated with Cardiganshire (Dyfed) and is the pride of that county. It has not been proved but it is possible that the Welsh Cob is at the base of America's Morgan Horse. Early representatives of this last breed showed a marked resemblance to the Welsh Cob and were possessed of many of the qualities for which the Cob is famous.

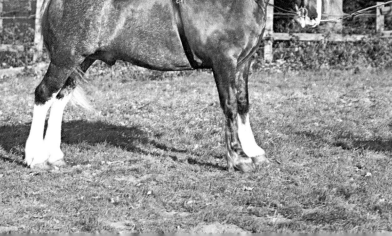

Ireland

Connemara

Appearance A strongly built, attractive pony of distinctive riding type. Well proportioned with good legs and feet.
Height 13–14 hh.
Colour Dun, but also grey, black, bay and brown.
Temperament and characteristics A tough, hard pony of good constitution. Intelligent and kind. A natural jumper and cross-country pony.
Uses A riding pony, very suitable for children but big enough for adults. Also an excellent cross with Thoroughbred to produce hunters and competition horses.
Origin The western seaboard of Ireland. The Connemara is indigenous to Ireland and may share a common ancestry with the Western Isles ponies. Spanish blood was certainly introduced in the 1500s from the wrecked Armada but more recently the breed was improved by the Connemara Society's purchase of two small Thoroughbreds and one part-Arab stallion. One of the former was Little Heaven, sire of the showjumper Dundrum out of a native mare.

Irish Draught

Appearance A heavy, strong, clean-legged, light working horse, giving an impression of rugged strength. Deep-bodied on short legs.
Height 15–16 hh.
Colour Bay, brown, chestnut, grey.
Temperament and characteristics Sensible, enduring and intelligent. An active horse but not a galloper.
Uses Originally as a working horse but, more importantly, as the foundation for the Irish Hunter.
Origin Ireland. An indigenous working breed probably developed from the Connemara and grown bigger on better pastures in the south. Unfortunately, although efforts are being made to preserve these useful horses, they are not now to be found in large numbers.

France

Anglo-Arab

Appearance Elegant saddle horse of the best riding type.
Height 16–13·3 hh.
Colour Bay, brown and chestnut are the most common.
Temperament and characteristics Anglo-Arabs, hopefully, combine the best of both Arab and Thoroughbred. They have the scope and some of the speed of the latter but without the Thoroughbred's excitable temperament, and they retain much of the Arab's qualities of soundness, endurance and stamina.
Uses Ideal competition horses in all riding disciplines.
Origin Bred throughout the world but recognized as a breed in France, where they are bred extensively at the studs of Pompadour, Tarbes, Gelos and Pau. The modern French Anglo is a mix of three elements: Arab, Thoroughbred and Anglo-Arab. The dam may be any of these so long as the progeny possesses 25 per cent Arab blood. There are, therefore, numerous possible permutations. The best of the French Anglos, including many Olympic medal-winning horses, show between 25 and 45 per cent Arabian blood. The general practice in France is to mate an Arab stallion to a mare of Thoroughbred or mixed blood, most of these sires being imported from Tunisia and Syria.

Ardennais

Appearance A short, thick-set draught horse, close to the ground and very compact. Very strong and muscular with massive bone structure.
Height 15·3 hh.
Colour Bay, roan, chestnut.
Temperament and characteristics Exceptionally calm and easy to handle, and a willing, hard worker. Hardy and tough.
Uses All forms of draught.
Origin Ardennes region of France and Belgium. *See* Belgian Ardennes.

Auxois

Appearance Strong draught horse with legs relatively free from feather. Similar to the Trait du Nord and Ardennais.
Height 15·2–16 hh.
Colour Bay or red roan.
Temperament and characteristics Quiet, kind and willing. Very hardy.
Uses Heavy draught.
Origin Burgundy, France. This is the old Burgundian heavy which has existed since the Middle Ages, when it was probably lighter, smaller and more active. Present-day Auxois are the result of 19th-century crossings with Percheron and Boulonnais stallions and later crossings with the Ardennais. Most Auxois horses today have a quantity of Ardennais blood but much attention is paid to the maintenance of type and colour.

Boulonnais

Appearance A heavy draught of unusually elegant appearance, well rounded and proportioned, and majestic in outlook. Very like the Percheron.
Height 16–16·3 hh.
Colour Grey, but chestnut and bay are preferred.
Temperament and characteristics A gay, intelligent, gentle horse that shows, if in a different form, its debt to Oriental blood.
Uses Heavy draught.
Origin Northern France. The breed derives from the ancient heavy horse of northern Europe and is said to have its first infusion of Eastern blood from the horses of the Numidian cavalry stationed on the Boulogne coast before Caesar's invasion of Britain. The Crusades and the Spanish occupation of Flanders brought more Oriental blood, which is still evident in the breed, and also a little Andalucian.

Breton

Appearance A hairy little draught horse reminiscent of the primitive Steppe Horse and with a very pony look about it.

Height Average 15 hh, depending upon type.

Colour Red and blue roan, chestnut, bay.

Temperament and characteristics Lively disposition but good natured and willing. Despite various outcrosses, it has retained its own particular character.

Uses Draught and carriage, depending on type. An ideal subject for improving primitive types and bringing them closer to a draught animal.

Origin Brittany, France. The indigenous horse of the north-west of France. Three types have evolved: the Draught Breton, produced by outcrosses with the Boulonnais, Ardennais, and Percheron; the Postier, deriving from Norfolk and Hackney crossings which have given it a smart, energetic trotting pace; and the Corlay, a carriage horse which may also be ridden. The Corlay, the product of outcrosses to Arabs and Thoroughbreds, is now rarely seen and may, indeed, be virtually extinct.

Camargue

Appearance A large, straight-headed horse with a short neck and often with poor, upright shoulders, but with great depth of girth, good back and loins. Tail low set, bone good, and the feet, though large, are hard. Luxuriant mane and tail.

Height Not above 15 hh.

Colour Silky white.

Temperament and characteristics Independent but fiery and courageous. The action is peculiar, the walk being long and high stepping, while the trot appears stilted and unnatural. The gallop is free. Very hardy, thriving on poor fare, very enduring, agile, and sure footed.

Uses The mount of the *gardians* (Camargue cowboys) in their work with the black bulls of the Camargue. Also for tourist-trekking.

Origin The Camargue, France. The Camargue is descended from Asian or Mongol horses on which barbarians (the Ostrogoths and Vandals) invaded Europe. It may be a distant cousin of the Berber, to which it bears some resemblance. All these have played a part in the evolution but it is just as probable that a horse native to these areas existed 50 000 years ago. Skeletal deposits dated at being of that age were discovered at Solutre, in the Charollais region, and these remains of European wild horses are remarkably similar in structure and detail to the present Camargue. Clearly, there must also have been Spanish and Oriental blood involved but there has been no recourse to outside blood in recent times.

Charollais Halfbred

Appearance A strong, hunter type of horse.
Height 15—16·2 hh.
Colour All solid colours.
Temperament and characteristics Sensible, workman-like and sound.
Uses Formerly a cavalry remount, now a general sporting horse.
Origin France. A product of Thoroughbred and Anglo-Norman blood, it is known under the collective heading of Demi-Sang Charollais, together with the Nivernais and Bourbonnais halfbreds. The three types are very similar.

Comtois

Appearance A light draught horse. Straight neck, large head, a long back and a tendency to cow hocks.
Height 14·3—15·3 hh.
Colour Bay, chestnut.
Temperament and characteristics Active and willing, hardy and sure footed with the quick, lively movement of the mountain-bred.
Uses Light draught.
Origin Franche-Comté, the Franco-Swiss borderland. The horse is particularly suited to work in this hilly region where, it is said, it has been since the 500s A.D. It was used as a warhorse, but more frequently for transport purposes, in the Middle Ages.

French Saddle Horse (*Selle Français*) — (Anglo-Norman, Norman)

Appearance Strong, hunter type of quality, perhaps a little long in the leg but with good bone.
Height 15·2—16·3 hh.
Colour Any, but usually chestnut.
Temperament and characteristics An equable temperament allied to strength and good conformation. A competition horse well suited for eventing, show-jumping, and other activities.
Uses Competitive sports.
Origin France. French Saddle Horse is a term only introduced in 1965 and the stud book is a continuation of the former Anglo-Norman one. It covers the Norman and Anglo-Norman breeds which derive from the same root but which are not, in fact, identical. Indeed, the Norman comprises two very different types, one a riding horse and one a draught cob. The Norman horses descend from a heavy draught type of the same name that existed 1000 years ago. This horse was a war-horse and, when it became outmoded, it developed into a lighter, working horse during the 1500s and 1600s. The introduction of German blood and, to a degree that of Arabs and Berbers, produced a strong riding horse. Nineteenth-century imports of English Thoroughbreds, Norfolk Trotters and hunter-type stallions led to the Anglo-Norman which is now very Thoroughbred in type.

French Trotter (*Demi-Sang* Trotter)

Appearance A tough-looking, raw-boned, rather tall horse, well coupled with the characteristic sloping quarters of the trotting horse.
Height About 16·2 hh.
Colour Black, bay, chestnut, roan, and grey.
Temperament and characteristics Willing and courageous. Bigger than the usual trotter, the *Demi-Sang* also races, at trot, under saddle.
Uses Racing trotter in harness and under saddle.
Origin France. An offshoot from the Anglo-Norman, developed from Norfolk Trotter blood in the 1800s. Other outcrosses have been to the Orlov Trotters and the American but since 1941 the breed has remained pure. Trotting in France is just as popular as flat-racing and some 6000 races are held each year.

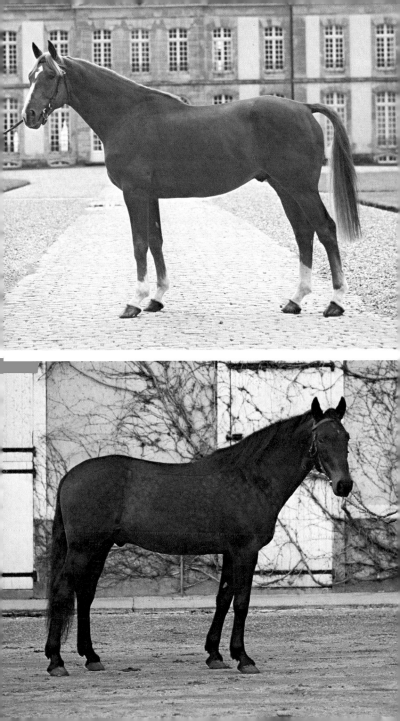

Landais

Appearance   A slightly-built pony with a small head but otherwise of unimpressive conformation.
Height   About 12 hh.
Colour   Grey.
Origin   Landes, France. A semi-wild pony living in the Landes forests. It is close to the pony of the Chalosse plains, near the Adour river, and to the Barthais pony, living on the marshes of the Adour. It is, however, smaller than either.

Limousin Halfbred

Appearance   A quality horse showing marked Arabian characteristics.
Height   About 16 hh.
Colour   Usually chestnut or bay.
Temperament and characteristics   A lively, gay horse of good temperament.
Uses   A general sporting horse.
Origin   France. The Limousin shares the same regional group, the Demi-Sang du Centre, as the Charollais Halfbred and all these good French halfbreds come under the general title of Cheval de Selle Français (not the same as the Anglo-Norman). The Limousin Halfbred has been developed on the foundation of the old, rather strong, Limousin mares mixed, over a century or more, with Thoroughbred, Arab and Anglo-Arab blood. The result is a horse resembling the Anglo-Arab but showing more of its Oriental antecedents. Some of the modern Limousins have some Anglo-Norman blood as well.

Merens (sometimes known as Ariègeois)

Appearance Stocky, heavy headed pony with luxurious mane and tail. A little like a British Dales Pony but coarser.
Height About 13·3 hh.
Colour Black.
Temperament and characteristics Tough and semi-wild, a mountain pony.
Uses Suitable for hill farming.
Origin The high foothills of the Ariège, France. An ancient, possibly indigenous pony with Oriental background.

Percheron

Appearance A heavy horse of beautiful proportions with a fine head denoting its debt to Arabian blood. A big but graceful horse.
Height 15·2–17 hh (average about 16·1 hh).
Colour Grey and black.
Temperament and characteristics A more sensitive horse than the other heavy breeds, demanding tactful handling but more rewarding in its response. The Percheron, probably the most popular of the world's heavies, has a much freer movement than is usual in heavy horses, even being able to show extension at trot. The breed is noted for its stamina and endurance.
Uses Heavy draught.
Origin The Perche region, France. The true Percheron Stud Book is confined to horses bred in the Departments of Sarthe, Eure-et-Loir, Loir-et-Cher, and Orne; all others have to have their own books. It originates from a cross between Norman and Arab horses in very early times. Later it was crossed with heavier draught breeds and with a little more Arab blood. Percherons have been exported all over the world and are particular favourites in America. The British Percheron, centred round the fen country of Cambridgeshire, has been bred so as to lose the feather round the legs and has been crossed with Thoroughbreds to produce heavyweight hunters, often from a second cross.

Poitevin

Appearance Large and heavy, exhibiting every equine conformational fault.
Height 16·2–17 hh.
Colour Dun, sometimes bay or brown.
Temperament and characteristics Dull, lethargic, and unintelligent. A poor workhorse because of its physical and mental limitations.
Uses The Poitevin is also known as Mulassiers, which indicates the one useful contribution they are able to make – the mares breed the huge Poitevin mules which are much in demand, particularly in America. The Poitevin mares are put to the *baudets du Poitou*, large jackasses, to produce these valuable animals.
Origin Poitou, France. The horse, of northern origin (The Netherlands, Denmark, Norway), was imported originally for the job of draining marshlands. Coming from similar, flat, swampy areas, its huge, round feet are well adapted for this work.

Trait du Nord

Appearance Similar to the Ardennais, of which it is an 1800s off-shoot, but larger and heavier. Very heavy head and a low-set tail. Legs not excessively feathered.
Height 16 hh.
Colour Bay, chestnut, roan.
Temperament and characteristics Gentle and easily managed. Very strong and hardy.
Uses Heavy draught.
Origin North-east France. An offshoot of the Ardennais, it contains crosses of Belgian and Dutch Draught.

The Netherlands

Dutch Draught

Appearance A massive horse very similar to its ancestor, the Brabant.
Height Up to 16·3 hh.
Colour Chestnut, bay, grey, and sometimes black.
Temperament and characteristics A quiet horse with a turn of speed and great stamina.
Uses Heavy draught.
Origin The Netherlands. The Dutch Draught was created after 1918 for work on mixed farms on sandy soil as well as for heavier work on arable farms. Zeeland-type mares were crossed with Brabant stallions and to a lesser degree with the Belgian Ardennais to produce the Dutch Draught.

Friesian Horse

Appearance A strong, muscular horse with a long, fine head carried high. Short, powerful legs, with tremendous bone and with feather on the lower parts. Hard, blue feet.
Height 15 hh.
Colour Black with no white markings.
Temperament and characteristics Hard, cheerful worker and of a kind disposition, but sensitive and so requiring intelligent handling. High action at the trot.
Uses An all-round working horse and a most popular harness horse. Used also in circuses.
Origin Friesland, the Netherlands. The Friesian is one of the oldest breeds in Europe and in its native land excites feelings akin to those experienced by the British, particularly the townsmen, when they see teams of Shire horses in the show ring or working in the city streets. The Friesian stems from the 'cold-blooded' heavy horses that survived the Ice Age; a domestic heavy horse existed in Friesland 3000 years ago. Over the centuries, Oriental and particularly Andalucian blood, during and following the Eighty Years War, was added to the Friesian. In time, as trotting races became popular, a lighter, faster horse was bred which was not so suitable for utility purposes and the breed went into decline. In 1913 there were only three stallions in Friesland but the breed, with the help of the Oldenburg, survived and now flourishes in its native country.

Gelderland

Appearance A typical, upstanding carriage horse of some presence. Well made and standing on short, strong legs. A plain head with a convex face.
Height 15·2–16 hh.
Colour Chestnut and grey are the most common, but some skewbalds occur.
Temperament and characteristics Docile, strong and active with good movement.
Uses Light draught, agriculture, carriage work. Modern Gelderlanders are also ridden. They are not fast but are said to jump well.
Origin Gelderland, the Netherlands. A very popular harness horse in the Netherlands, the Gelderland came into being over 100 years ago when native mares were put to stallions from Britain, notably Norfolk Roadsters, and from Egypt (Arabs) as well as to horses from Germany, Hungary, Poland and Russia. As a type became fixed, Oldenburg and East Friesians were used as well as Hackneys. Since then there has been an outcross to Anglo-Norman.

Groningen

Appearance Similar to the Oldenburg.
Height 15·2–16 hh.
Colour Black, bay, dark brown, often with white markings.
Temperament and characteristics Strong, enduring, quiet and willing. Stylish action.
Uses A carriage horse.
Origin Groningen, the Netherlands. An offshoot of the Oldenburg, the breed derives from crossing the latter and the East Friesian with the heavy Friesian mares. The breed is now rare and may even no longer exist in its pure form.

Belgium

Belgian Ardennes

Appearance Compact, stocky animal with a huge barrel, very crested neck, wide and deep chest and exceptionally massive, short legs with much feather. Big head with a broad face.
Height 15·1–15·3 hh.
Colour Bay, roan, chestnut.
Temperament and characteristics Very kind, willing and gentle. Well-suited to work in hilly country and an economical feeder.
Uses Heavy draught.
Origin Ardennes area of Belgium and France. This is the oldest of the two Belgian heavy breeds and many continental draught breeds are descended from the Ardennes. The Ardennes was mentioned by Caesar in *De Bello Gallico* and praised as a tireless worker. The modern breed has been influenced by the Brabant.

Brabant (Belgian Heavy Draught)

Appearance Massive, imposing, and handsome with a pronounced square head which is proportionately small. Very deep girth, short back. Short, strong legs with much feather.
Height 16·1–17 hh.
Colour Red roan, chestnut, sometimes bay, dun, brown and grey.
Temperament and characteristics Good tempered with a markedly active walk.
Uses Heavy draught.
Origin Belgium, covering Flanders, Anvers, Brabant, Hainaut, Limburg, Liège, Namur, and Luxembourg. Originally the Flanders Horse, the breed was produced by a severe selective process which resulted in three distinct lines: Gros de la Dendre, Gris du Hainaut, and Colosses de la Mehaigue. Brabant blood has been used to improve many continental heavy breeds and 'Flanders' stallions contributed to British heavy breeds, in particular the Clydesdale.

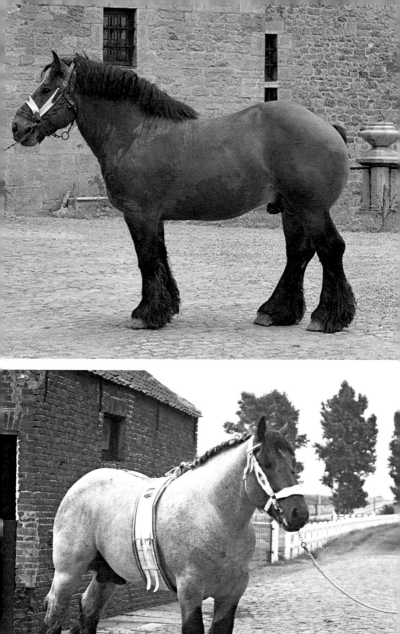

Germany

Bavarian Warm Blood

Appearance A heavyweight riding horse.
Height About 16 hh.
Colour Chestnut.
Temperament and characteristics A very temperate horse, great consideration being given to this quality in its breeding. An enduring, solid horse if not an exciting one.
Uses A heavyweight riding horse also fitted for farm work.
Origin Lower Bavaria, Germany. The Bavarian Warm Blood was originally the chestnut warhorse of the Rott valley, the renowned Rottaler, the name being changed only recently. The Rottaler was well known at the time of the Crusades and, by the 1500s, was being bred systematically. In the 1700s British halfbred hunter stallions were imported; Cleveland Bays and horses from Zweibrucken and Normandy were also used. At the end of the 1600s the Oldenburg was introduced to give greater substance to the breed.

Dulmen

Appearance Somewhat mixed, resembling to some degree the ponies running in the New Forest, although there is no link between the two.
Height About 12·3 hh.
Colour Any.
Temperament and characteristics Semi-wild.
Uses None specifically.
Origin Westphalia, Germany. The ponies, it is claimed, have run in the Meerfelder Bruch since 1316. They are the property of the Duke of Croy and unwanted stock are sold annually. Stallions have been imported from Poland and Britain and the breed is not, therefore, pure. It is however, one of Germany's two native ponies, the other being the Senner Pony, and both contributed to the origin of the Hanoverian. The Senner Pony is now near extinction if it has not already disappeared. It was an incredibly tough specimen that ran wild in the Teutoberg Forest of Hanover.

East Friesian

Appearance A quality horse, similar to the Oldenburg but lighter and more 'blood'-like.

Height 16–16·2 hh.

Colour Any solid colour.

Temperament and characteristics Spirited and courageous and possessed of free riding action.

Uses A refined saddle and carriage horse.

Origin Thuringia, East Germany. Up to World War II there was no difference between the East Friesian and the Oldenburg, exchange and interbreeding between the two provinces being easily accomplished. Now that this is no longer possible the East Friesian is developing along different lines. Refinement has been achieved by the use of Arabs (notably Wind Ox, Jason Ox, and Halali Ox) from the Marbach stud and from Hungary's Babolna stud, the use of the grey, Gazal, being particularly significant. (*See also* Oldenburg.)

German Trotter

Appearance A small horse with a pleasing head. Shoulder somewhat upright, quarters sloping away but well developed and deep in the girth. Legs and feet very hard.

Height About 15·3 hh.

Colour All solid colours.

Temperament and characteristics A bold, hard horse with qualities of endurance, speed, and stamina.

Uses Trotting racing.

Origin West Germany. Trotting is more popular and more highly developed in Germany than any other form of horse racing. The record for a German Trotter over 1000 metres (1100 yards) is held by Permit, by Epilog, a notable German Trotter sire, which covered the distance in 1 minute, 17·3 seconds. The German Trotter developed from the Russian Orlov Trotter but has been improved by the heavy use of American Standard breeds and more recently by the French Trotter.

Hanoverian

Appearance A strong, powerful horse of good proportions, sometimes a little plain.
Height 16·2–17 hh.
Colour Bay, brown chestnut, black.
Temperament and characteristics Intelligent, bold, and very athletic if not a great galloper when compared with the Thoroughbred.
Uses For many years a multipurpose horse, the modern Hanoverian is a riding horse with a particular talent for showjumping and dressage.
Origin Hanover and Lower Saxony, Germany. Initially developed from Oriental, Andalucian, and Neapolitan stallions crossed with the indigenous mares in the 1600s, the Hanoverian found royal patronage in the 1700s through the English Kings of the House of Hanover, George I and George II. In 1735 the latter founded the stallion depot at Celle. Foundation stock at the depot was a band of fourteen black Holstein stallions and later many English Thoroughbreds were used. The type of horse aimed for was a multipurpose one, strong enough for agricultural work and sufficiently elegant to be used as a carriage and driving horse. The emphasis changed after World War II in accordance with the new demand for a general sporting horse, and infusions of Trakehner (East Prussian) and Thoroughbred blood were made to this end. The Hanoverian is now Germany's leading warm blood and Hanoverian stallions are numerous throughout the country. The Westphalian horses are, in fact, Hanoverians in all but name even if they are known as Westfalisches Pferd.

Holstein

Appearance A somewhat heavier horse than the modern Hanoverian and like the latter very powerful in build. Very strong in the quarters and short legged.
Height 15·3–16·2 hh.
Colour Usually bay, black or brown.
Temperament and characteristics Sensible, intelligent and good natured. Versatile and willing.
Uses In former times a coach and carriage horse. Nowadays the Holstein is in an all-round riding horse and excels at showjumping, eventing, and dressage.
Origin Holstein, Germany. Like the Hanoverian, the Holstein was founded on indigenous mares crossed with imported stallions, the native stock tracing back to the heavy medieval warhorse. In the 1800s the breed was made lighter and improved by the Thoroughbred and by the old Yorkshire Coach Horse to become a dual-purpose carriage and riding horse. Since World War II the complexion has been changed radically by the heavy use of both German and English Thoroughbreds. The Holstein, like the Hanoverian, is now a competition horse and many of Germany's best showjumpers, including the great Meteor, are Holsteins.

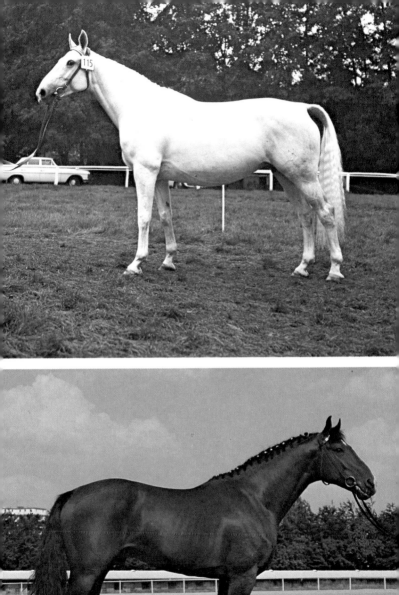

Mecklenburg

Appearance Essentially a smaller version of the Hanoverian.
Height 15·2–16·3 hh.
Colour All solid colours.
Temperament and characteristics A steady, reliable saddle horse, very easily managed.
Uses Between the wars, it was a cavalry remount; today it is an all-purpose saddle horse.
Origin East Germany. Much the same bloodlines have been used in the development of the Mecklenburg as in the Hanoverian and the two are very closely related. It seems likely, now that the interchange of stock between the two parts of modern Germany is difficult, that the Mecklenburg will develop on its own lines and, following the Hanoverian example, use Thoroughbred blood in greater proportions.

Oldenburg

Appearance A tall horse, heaviest of the German warm bloods and rather more plain. Excellent bone, very strong in the back and, although tall, the deep body is set on short legs.
Height 16·2–17·2 hh.
Colour Mostly black, bay and brown.
Temperament and characteristics A steady, bold horse. It matures very much earlier than other German breeds which is surprising in a horse of such massive frame.
Uses Initially a strong coach horse, the breed, as in other cases, is now a riding horse although it still retains its harness ability.
Origin Oldenburg and East Friesland, Germany. The Oldenburg based on the Friesian was established in the early 1600s. In the 1700s, Spanish, Neapolitan, Barb, and English Thoroughbreds were used, and a hundred years after that there was an importation of more Thoroughbred blood together with Cleveland Bay, Hanoverian, and Norman. The result was a strong, temperate coach horse. When the need changed after 1945 towards a riding horse, the Oldenburg changed in type again. A Norman stallion, Condor, and the Thoroughbred, Lupus, were used. After them came more Thoroughbreds, some Hanoverians and a number of Trakehners. Despite these introductions, or rather because of them, the Oldenburg is extremely level in breed type.

Rhineland Heavy Draught

Appearance A square· exceptionally bulky horse. Very powerful and low to the ground.
Height 16–17 hh.
Colour Chestnut or red roan with black points, with flaxen mane and tail.
Temperament and characteristics Good natured. An early maturing horse which, because of its short legs, is capable of great traction.
Uses Heavy draught.
Origin The Rhineland, Germany. Until recent years, the Rhenish horse was to be found in all sorts of forms all over Germany, and often under different names. The breed shares the same ancestors as the Belgian Draught and at least one noted authority suggests that its origin, like that of the latter, goes back to the Ardennes Horse and from there to the prehistoric diluvial horse. The Niedersachsen Heavy Draught of Lower Saxony is one of the Rhineland types and still exists, though in small and decreasing numbers.

Trakehner (East Prussian)

Appearance A quality horse of excellent conformation with many Thoroughbred characteristics.
Height 16–16·2 hh.
Colour All solid colours.
Temperament and characteristics A delightfully dispositioned horse, spirited but tractable and usually a good jumper. Enduring and of great stamina.
Uses Formerly a cavalry remount with the ability to do agricultural work, the Trakehner is now an excellent riding horse.
Origin Germany, east Prussia (now Poland). The Trakehner stud was founded in 1732 by King Friedrich Wilhelm I. At the beginning of the 1800s outcrosses were made to the Arab but thereafter English Thoroughbreds were used almost exclusively. By 1913 no less than 84·3 per cent of the mares were by Thoroughbred stallions. In 1945, 1200 of the 25 000 registered Trakehners reached what is now West Germany from east Prussia after a journey lasting three months. The breed is now bred privately in West Germany and is still popular and numerous in Poland. The Polish Masuren is, in fact, the East Prussian or Trakehner under another name.

Schleswig Heavy Draught

Appearance A compact, cob-like draught horse with a plain convex-profiled head. A tendency towards an over-long, over-flat barrel and towards soft and flat feet is noticeable in some specimens.

Height 15·2—16 hh.

Colour Predominantly chestnut but also bay and grey.

Temperament and characteristics A willing worker of quiet disposition with a more lively movement than is usual in heavy breeds because of the presence of Thoroughbred blood.

Uses Draught, farm work and urban transport.

Origin Schleswig-Holstein, Germany. The breed can be traced to the Jutland Horse of Denmark to which, in the 1800s, Yorkshire Coach Horse and Thoroughbred blood was introduced. Dependence upon Danish stallions continued up to World War II but afterwards outcrosses were made to the Boulonnais and the Breton in an effort to counteract the failings of the breed, that is, the slab sides and the soft feet.

Württemberg Horse

Appearance A big cob. Compact, deep and strong with good feet and a plain head.

Height About 16 hh.

Colour Black, bay, brown, chestnut.

Temperament and characteristics A hardy, unassuming horse, easily handled and economical to keep.

Uses A harness and riding cob suitable for work on small mountain farms.

Origin Württemberg, Germany. A product of the famous Marbach stud, the early Württemberg was the result of crossing the indigenous mares with the Arabs for which Marbach is famous. To give greater strength, East Prussian and Norman stallions were used and to a lesser degree Oldenburgs, Nonius, and even Suffolks and Clydesdales, the last two without much success. Finally, the Württemberg in the form desired was achieved by an Anglo-Norman stallion, of the cob type, a horse called Faust. Recently improvement has been effected through East Prussian horses, particularly a sire called Julmond.

Switzerland

Einsiedler (Swiss Anglo-Norman)

Appearance A strong saddle horse, powerfully built, the deep body carried on short, strong legs.
Height 15·3–16·2 hh
Colour All solid colours.
Temperament and characteristics A steady, sensible horse, sound and versatile.
Uses A dual-purpose riding and driving horse, suitable for cavalry and all general purposes.
Origin Switzerland. The breed takes its name from the stud at Kloster Einsiedel with which it is principally associated. It is also known as the Swiss Anglo-Norman, and derives largely from the French horse of this name. There is evidence of some Hackney blood but Anglo-Normans have been bred in Switzerland for some centuries.

Franches-Montagnes

Appearance A small, very strong, agricultural horse, big-topped on short legs. A heavy, cob-type horse, a little reminiscent of the Welsh Cob.
Height 15 hh.
Colour Most colours including roan but no part-colours.
Temperament and characteristics A very active, sure-footed horse of good temperament, able to work in hill country and very versatile in other respects.
Uses An all-round agricultural horse which was also much in demand for military draught.
Origin The Jura, Switzerland. The breed evolved about 100 years ago as the result of crossing native mares with Anglo-Norman stallions and there were also infusions of English halfbred hunter stallion blood and a little of the Ardennes. Since then, the breed has remained pure.

Freiberger

Appearance An elegant saddle horse of light to middle weight with some pronounced Arabian characteristics, but possessed of bone and some substance.
Height 15·2—16 hh.
Colour All solid colours.
Temperament and characteristics A bright, intelligent horse, enduring and with ample stamina.
Uses A saddle horse.
Origin Switzerland, developed at the stud at Avenches. The base of the breed is the old cold-blood Freiberger or Tura, the Franches-Montagnes, to which has been added Norman blood and a great deal of Shagya Arab from the Babolna stud in Hungary. There is now little trace of the cold-blood ancestry except in the bone and general substance.

Austria

Haflinger

Appearance A strong, heavy pony. The back somewhat long, but very strong in the loins. Short legs with ample bone and with feather on the extremities.
Height 13·3 hh.
Colour Chestnut with flaxen mane and tail.
Temperament and characteristics Docile, very strong, hardy, capable of much work and not requiring high feeding. Sure footed. Very long lived, some reputed to be in work at forty years old.
Uses All types of harness and pack work, and can be ridden.
Origin The Etschlander Mountains near Meran (Hafling mountain district) of Austria and Bavaria. Breed centre is the village of Jenesien. Considered to be a cold-blood and probably descended from the Alpine Heavy Horse and adapted to mountain work. Both Oriental and Norik blood have been used. Young stock are raised on mountain pasture, a practice known as *alpung* (alping) and one which has contributed to the development of this active mountain pony. The founder of the modern breed is recognized as the Arab, El Bedavi, through a halfbred grandson, El Bedavi XXII, from whom all Haflingers descend. The brand mark is an Edelweiss with an H in the centre.

Lipizzaner

Appearance The modern Lipizzaner is small, compact, and almost cobby, showing both Arab and Andalucian character.
Height About 15·2 hh.
Colour White with an occasional bay. (Foals are born black, grey, or brown and change colour over a period of about seven to ten years.)
Temperament and characteristics Equable and intelligent. Very strong in the back and quarters, and the well-ribbed body is set on short, strong legs.
Uses Primarily a High School horse but greatly used in harness.
Origin The Spanish School stud at Piber, Austria but also bred extensively in Czechoslovakia, Hungary, Yugoslavia, and Rumania. The breed is inevitably associated with the Spanish Riding School of Vienna, where the art of classical riding has been practised consistently for over 400 years. The breed derives its name from the village of Lipizza in the Karst country in the north-west of Yugoslavia. A stud was founded here by the Archduke Charles in 1580 from imported Spanish (Andalucian) horses. Up to the 1600s the stud relied upon pure Spanish imports and later, as the source diminished, to closely related strains. The most significant outcross was in about the year 1816 when the grey Arabian, Siglavy, was used to found an important Lipizzaner line.

Norik Horse (South German Cold Blood)

Appearance A plain, medium-sized, working horse with a heavy head. Short, thick, neck, upright shoulder, long barrelled and wide chested. Clean legs and good feet.
Height 16—16·2 hh.
Colour Bay, chestnut, brown.
Temperament and characteristics Docile, sure footed and with good action.
Uses A cold-blood draught horse.
Origin Austria and throughout Bavaria and south Germany where it is known as the South German Cold Blood. The Norik has its very early origin in the kingdom of Noricum, a vassal state of the Roman Empire which corresponded very closely with the borders of present-day Austria. Its probable descent is from the Haflinger but from 1565 onwards Spanish, Neapolitan and Burgundian bloods were used to improve the breed and give it greater size. A strain of Norik Horse, the spotted Pinzgauer, used to be a separate breed as did the Bavarian Oberlander; both, however, are now incorporated into the main Norik breed.

Czechoslovakia

Kladruber

Appearance An impressive, upstanding horse, handsome but not a quality sort. A taller version of the Andalucian with a similar convex face.
Height 16·2–17·2 hh.
Colour Predominantly grey but also black.
Temperament and characteristics Steady, good-natured horse.
Uses At one time, when the breed was larger in size, exclusively a coach and carriage horse. Today, the Kladruber is still a harness horse but is used to produce agricultural horses and crossbreeds suitable for riding. The latter cannot claim to be very successful except in dressage, for which their quiet temperament makes them suitable.
Origin Kladruby in Bohemia, Czechoslovakia. A stud, based on Spanish horses, was founded at Kladruby in 1572 by Maximilian II and provided the coach horses for the Imperial carriages. By the beginning of the 1800s only black and grey horses were bred and the breed then averaged 18 hh. The stock, at times much interbred, was refreshed by the import of Neapolitans and by exchange between Kladruby and other state studs, but it was not until a cross was tried in 1921 with a Shagya Arabian that a successful outcross was made. Since 1918, the Kladruber has become smaller and more active. Only grey horses are now bred at Kladruby, the blacks being housed at another stud in the immediate neighbourhood. Kladrubers are still used on state occasions.

Hungary

Furioso (Furioso-North Star)

Appearance A handsome saddle/carriage horse of quality and substance. The tail is somewhat low set and the quarters slope away from the croup.
Height About 16 hh.
Colour Black, dark brown.
Temperament and characteristics A tractable, intelligent, versatile horse with a slightly exaggerated action.
Uses A riding horse of sufficient quality to be a good performer in all disciplines including steeplechasing at the standard reached in central European countries. Also used in harness.
Origin The Mezohegyes stud, Hungary. The breed was established in the 1800s from Norius-type mares and the two English foundation sires the Thoroughbred Furioso (1836) and the Norfolk Roadster, North Star (1844). Thereafter, more Thoroughbreds were used, notably Vibar, son of Buccaneer, the 1892 Ascot Gold Cup winner, Dante, and Nagyvezer.

Gidran Arabian

Appearance Arabian.
Height About 15 hh.
Colours All common to the Arab.
Temperament and characteristics Arabian.
Uses As breeding stock, competition horses and also driven to carriages.
Origin Hungary. The Gidran Arab is not pure and is frequently considered as an Anglo-Arab. There are two types: the heavier middle European often used for driving and the lighter southern and eastern type which is closer to its pure Arabian forebears. The Gidran is founded on Siglavy-Gidran imported from Arabia in 1816. He was chestnut and described as very tempestuous .

Murakoz

Appearance A draught horse showing considerably more quality than is usual in heavy breeds.
Height About 16 hh.
Colour Normally chestnut with flaxen mane and tail, but also bay, brown, black and grey.
Temperament and characteristics Even-tempered horses of strong constitution and economical feeders. Fast moving.
Uses Heavy agriculture.
Origin Neighbourhood of Hungary bordering the river Mura (also bred in Poland and Yugoslavia). The breed has developed during this century from native mares that were sometimes known as Mur-Insulan, crossed with Ardennais, Percheron, and Noriker stallions as well as with some Hungarian stallions of quality. In 1925, over 20 per cent of all the horses in Hungary were Murakozi but after World War II the stock was much depleted and it is now unlikely that the breed will regain its former eminence.

Nonius

Appearance Medium to heavyweight build of riding/carriage horse of two types.
Height Large — 15·3 hh and above; small — under 15·3 hh.
Colour Black, bay, dark brown.
Temperament and characteristics Calm, willing horse, very hard. Matures late and is noted for its longevity.
Uses Agriculture, ridden sports and harness. Crossed with Thoroughbreds it produces good quality competition horses of greater scope than itself.
Origin Mezohegyes stud, Hungary. (Also bred in Yugoslavia, Rumania, and Czechoslovakia.) The forerunner of the Furioso, the Nonius was founded by Nonius Senior, a horse foaled in Calvados, France in 1810 and said to be by an English halfbred out of a Norman mare. He produced fifteen notable stallions from mares of different breeds ranging from Arab to Anglo-Norman and by 1890 his registered descendants numbered some 2800 stallions and over 3000 mares.

Shagya-Arabian

Appearance 'Dry' classical Arabian type.
Height About 15 hh.
Colour As those common to the Arab.
Temperament and characteristics Arabian.
Uses Breeding purposes, riding, and cavalry horses, harness horses.
Origin Babolna stud, Hungary. The Shagya, although indistinguishable from the purebred Arab, is not technically of pure blood because the foundation mares are regarded as having been impure or of insufficiently recorded descent. Shagya, after which the Hungarian Arab is named, was imported from Syria in 1836 following an outbreak of disease at Babolna.

Poland

Hucul

Appearance A powerful, primitive pony resembling its ancestor the Tarpan, particularly about the head.
Height 12·1–13·1 hh.
Colour Usually dun or bay but piebalds are common.
Temperament and characteristics Sensible and very docile. Very hardy.
Uses The standard workhorse for farmers in southern Poland and the Carpathians. Much used in harness.
Origin Carpathian Mountains, Poland. The Hucul probably descends directly from the Stone Age Tarpan and there have been ponies of this Hucul type in the Carpathians for thousands of years. Arab blood has been used for the improvement of the breed within the past century.

Konik

Appearance Like the Hucul, the Konik is an important example of the Tarpan descendants but it is much more a little horse than a pony (*Konik* means small horse). There is a hint of Arab blood.
Height About 13 hh.
Colour All shades of dun.
Temperament and characteristics Easily managed, tough, hardy and willing. Works hard and long on minimum rations.
Uses A multipurpose 'horse' for small farmers.
Origin Poland. It is bred selectively at the Popielno and Jezewice studs and by numerous small farmers. Like the Hucul, the breed descends from the Tarpan and has been improved by the Arab.

Malapolski

Appearance Similar to the Wielkopolski but lighter and of greater quality.
Height Around 15·2 hh, but can be bigger according to type.
Colour All solid colours.
Temperament and characteristics Very quiet disposition and sound, with great stamina.
Uses The breed has only been developed in recent years and so there is still a variation in type according to the region in which the horses are bred. The best are very good riding horses and with their predominantly Oriental outlook must resemble the original Polish Horse. The largest type, the Sadecki, can be used for draught and has been influenced by the Hungarian Furioso. The Darbowsko-Tarnowski, another important type, has much Gidran blood.
Origin Southwest Poland.

Sokolsky

Appearance A light draught horse, very powerful, and with an unusual (in this type of horse) sloping shoulder. Large head with straight profile.
Height 15–16 hh.
Colour Usually chestnut.
Temperament and characteristics Calm, steady, easily managed. Good constitution and economical to keep.
Uses A working horse for small farmers.
Origin Poland, also bred in USSR. The horse stems from the Oldenburg crossed with native mares.

Tarpan (*Equus Przewalskii*)

Appearance 'Primitive'. Long head, convex face with a bulge around nostrils. Short neck, long back, sloping quarters.
Height About 13 hh.
Colour Mouse dun to brown with a dorsal stripe. Zebra bars on legs and sometimes on the body. Winter coat may be white. Dark mane and tail bordered with white hairs.
Temperament and characteristics Aggressive and brave when protecting young. A wild horse. Very fertile and nearly immune to disease.
Origin Poland. The last wild Tarpan is supposed to have been killed as long ago as 1879. The present herds were collected from peasant farms and placed in reserves by the Polish Government later in the same century. These horses may not be exact replicas of the original Tarpans but they are probably as close as makes no difference. The Tarpan represents the original Plateau Horse and with the Mongolian Wild Horse is a forerunner of all horses.

Wielkopolski

Appearance A compact, good-quality riding horse of strength and good conformation.
Height About 16 hh.
Colour All solid colours.
Temperament and characteristics Sensible, sound and tractable. Good mover and courageous.
Origin Poland. Wielkopolski is a composite name encompassing the Polish warm-blood horses, the Poznans, and the Mazurens (the East Prussian under its Polish name). All these are now regarded as one breed, Wielkopolski, although horses bred in particular districts like Mazury and Poznan, are recognized as being of distinct type. The new Wielkopolski will, therefore, in varying degrees carry the blood of Arabs, Hanoverians, Thoroughbreds, and East Prussians.

Portugal

(Besides the breeds described below, Portugal is noted for its excellent Garrano or Minho ponies, some of which have been improved by Arab blood, and which may have been among the foundation lines of the Andalucian (see page 102). Reared in the mountains of Garrano do Minho and Traz dos Mortes, the breed is of great antiquity and is shown in cave paintings of the Old Stone Age. Hardy and of fine conformation, with flowing mane and tail, the Garrano is from 10–12 hh and usually dark chestnut in colour.)

Altér Real

Appearance Similar to that of the Andalucian, particularly about the head and neck, but, if anything, a rather more finely drawn horse.
Height 15–16 hh.
Colour Bay, brown, sometimes grey. In former times chestnuts and piebalds were found.
Temperament and characteristics Courageous but highly strung and temperamental. The action is very extravagant with a lot of elevation in the knee and a corresponding lack of extension.
Uses A riding horse, especially suited to the Haute École.
Origin Portugal. The foundation was a band of selected Andalucians brought by the House of Braganza to the National stud at Vila de Portel in 1748. In the 1700s exhibitions of classical riding were given by the Altérs in the styles of the Renaissance and the breed flourished until 1821 when the French sacked the stud and the best horses were dispersed. Thereafter, the Altér was subjected to a variety of unsuitable crosses including a preponderance of Arabians. By 1910 the stud had been re-established by the purchase of Andalucian mares of the pure Zapata strain and some Spanish stallions, thus returning to the proven lines. In 1932 the stud came under the Ministry of Economy whose wise selective breeding resulted in the quality of the modern breed.

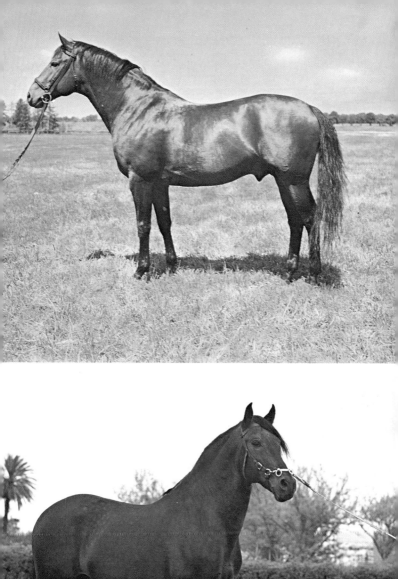

Lusitano

Appearance Very like the Andalucian with the characteristic head and the wavy mane and tail.
Height 15–16 hh.
Colour Usually grey.
Temperament and characteristics Highly courageous, responsive and intelligent. A very agile, athletic horse with the pronounced action of the Andalucian.
Uses A riding and parade horse, it is also the mount of the *rejoneadores*, the gentlemen bullfighters of Spain. The horses are trained to the highest level of the Haute Ecole and are exceedingly valuable.
Origin Portugal. The breed is old, having existed in Portugal for hundreds of years. Its base is without doubt the Andalucian but there have probably been Arabian outcrosses.

Spain

Andalucian

Appearance A noble horse with enormous presence. The neck is strong and in stallions crested, the head hawk-like in profile. The back is short and linked to broad quarters. The mane and tail are luxuriant and often wavy, the latter being set a little low.
Height About 15·2 hh.
Colour White, grey, bay or a characteristic mulberry shade.
Temperament and characteristics Agile, full of fire, but with a docile, friendly temperament. The action is spectacular. The Andalucian is a natural high stepper in front, often dishing.
Uses A riding horse with particular talents for 'school' disciplines.
Origin It seems very likely that the Andalucian came into being as a result of a crossing of Barb Horses with the indigenous stock during the various invasions of the Iberian peninsula. The native stock must themselves have been descended from north African horses which would have been able to cross into Iberia when the peninsula was still joined to north Africa by a strip of swampland. Up to the 1700s the Andalucian was without doubt the first horse of Europe and many of the European breeds were founded on the Spanish horses. The Lipizzaner is a virtually direct descendant together with the Frederiksborg, the Knabstrup and Kladruber. In America, even if the Andalucian influence is now far removed, the blood is represented in the Quarter Horse, the Appaloosa, the Saddle Horse, and others.

The Andalucian was the horse of the Renaissance and, therefore, at the root of the art of classical riding. Its descendants, the Lipizzaners, carry on that tradition and, in recent years, the Spanish School at Vienna has purchased a purebred Andalucian, Honoroso VI, from the Terry stud at Jerez de la Frontera, Spain.

In Spain itself there are some 1500 purebred Andalucians at the present, the main centres being at Seville, Cordoba, and Jerez. For centuries the great enthusiasts of the breed have been the Carthusian monks at Jerez and it is largely due to them that the Andalucian has been kept in a virtually pure form as the Andalucian-Carthusian.

Balearic Pony

Appearance Roman nosed, short necked, with an upright mane. Lightly built and lacking in bone.
Height 14 hh.
Colour Bay, brown.
Temperament and characteristics Exceptionally docile and willing.
Uses A farm and harness pony.
Origin Majorca. An old Mediterranean breed resembling horses depicted in ancient Greek art.

Hispano (Spanish Anglo-Arab)

Appearance A well-made, elegant saddle horse showing rather more Arabian characteristics than the average Anglo-Arab.
Height About 16 hh.
Colour Bay, chestnut, grey.
Temperament and characteristics A very agile, athletic horse, intelligent, spirited and highly courageous but of a tractable disposition.
Uses A saddle horse much favoured for competitive sport. Hispanos are also used for testing young bulls, their riders bringing the bull down with a long pole. If the bull is of the fighting sort he will rise and charge over and over again while horse and rider must avoid his rushes.
Origin Spain and Portugal. The Hispano is the result of Spanish Arabian mares bred to English Thoroughbreds, the best of the subsequent progeny sometimes being interbred.

Sorraia

Appearance Similar to both the Tarpan and the Asiatic Wild Horse in many respects. Primitive large head, generally poor conformation. Zebra markings often evident on the legs.
Height 12–13 hh.
Colour Generally dun.
Temperament and characteristics Tough, frugal pony.
Uses General utility.
Origin An indigenous pony, possibly related to the Garrano but not so much improved. It is to be found in both Spain and Portugal, north of Lisbon and along the Sorraia river into Spain.

Italy

Avelignese

Appearance Somewhat similar to the Haflinger to which it is related.
Height 13·3–14·2 hh.
Colour Chestnut with light mane and tail.
Temperament and characteristics A tough, long-lived mountain horse, docile and easily managed. Exceptionally sure of foot – a necessity for crossing the mountain trails on which it works.
Uses A draught and pack horse in the Alps and the Apennines.
Origin Central and northern Italy. The Avelignese has the same ancestors as the Haflinger which it resembles, both being descended from the extinct Avellinum-Haflinger. The Arab El Bedavi is thought to have had considerable influence on the breed.

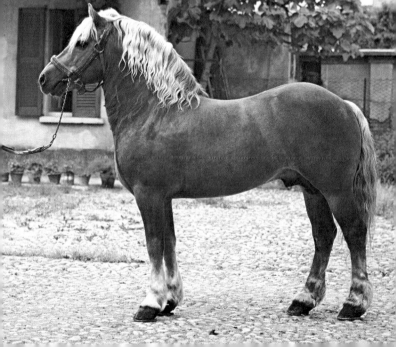

Calabrese

Appearance A medium-weight saddle horse of no particular distinction but usually well-made and with good shoulders and quarters.
Height About 16 hh.
Colour All colours.
Temperament and characteristics A straightforward horse with active movement. An average sort of saddle horse.
Uses Riding – a useful cavalry trooper.
Origin Calabria on the toe of Italy. There do not seem to be any distinctive breeding lines. The horses are bred under the aegis of the Italian States and the native stock have been improved by the use of Thoroughbreds.

Italian Heavy Draught

Appearance A heavy draught horse of striking coloration with a surprisingly fine head. The legs are hard but the joints are inclined to roundness and the feet are sometimes boxy.
Height 15–16 hh.
Colour Dark liver chestnut with light mane and tail. Also chestnut and roan.
Temperament and characteristics A kind, lively horse, capable of working at reasonable speed.
Uses Draught and meat.
Origin Central and northern Italy. This is, or was, the most popular draught horse in Italy. It derives from the Breton Horse and is, unfortunately, now bred more for the slaughterhouse than for any working purposes.

Maremmana (Maremma)

Appearance A heavy saddle horse. Common in appearance.
Height About 15·3 hh.
Colour All solid colours.
Temperament and characteristics Calm, steady horse, enduring and frugal.
Uses A saddle horse, favoured as a trooper, and useful for agricultural work. It is ridden to herd cattle by the Italian *butteri* (cowboys) and is used by mounted police.
Origin Italy. An indigenous horse relatively fixed in type despite a history of mixed breeding.

Salerno

Appearance A strong riding horse, the head showing the influence of its early Neopolitan ancestry.
Height About 16 hh.
Colour Any solid colour.
Temperament and characteristics Sensible and intelligent, it is a good utility horse with some pretensions as a jumper.
Uses Formerly the Italian cavalry horse, now less used in this respect but retained as a saddle horse.
Origin Mareninio and Salerno, Italy. The horse descends from the famous Neapolitan and it seems possible that its early foundation would have been the same as that of the Maremmana.

Sardinian

Appearance A small, tough-looking horse, with pronounced Oriental characteristics. The best have good conformation, but many exhibit the worst sort of faults.

Height 15–15·2 hh.

Colour Bay and brown.

Temperament and characteristics Hardy and enduring. Many of the breed are vicious and bad tempered, perhaps because of ill-treatment. The best type, properly handled, are bold and intelligent.

Uses A saddle horse for all purposes. With schooling the Sardinian is said to be able to jump well.

Origin Sardinia, Italy. The predominating influence is Oriental but no definitive origin of blood lines can be traced.

Yugoslavia

(Besides the Bosnian Pony described, which is nearest to being a native, Yugoslavia breeds numbers of Nonius, Lipizzaner, Arab, Belgian Draught and Norik. The Bosnian, however, represents 30 per cent of the horse population of about 1·3 million.)

Bosnian Pony

Appearance Compact mountain pony of Tarpan type. Very similar to the Polish Hucul.

Height 13–14·2 hh.

Colour Dun, brown, grey, black, chestnut.

Temperament and characteristics Very intelligent, tractable, tough and enduring.

Uses Mountain pack ponies, also used for light farm work and sometimes for riding.

Origin Bosnia, Herzegovina, Montenegro, Macedonia, and parts of Serbia, Yugoslavia. The breed originates from the Tarpan crossed with Steppe ponies such as the Asiatic Wild Horse and improved by Eastern blood introduced during the Turkish conquest. Much attention is paid to the breeding of the ponies and stallions before being used have to undergo a performance test carrying 100 kilogrammes (2 hundredweight) over 16 kilometres (10 miles). The distance has been covered in 1 hour 11 minutes.

In the better-cultivated areas of the north-west of Yugoslavia breeders have been able to produce a bigger pony of better quality. Although this pony stems from the same roots, it is called the Posovac.

Bulgaria

Danubian

Appearance A powerful, well-made animal sometimes giving the impression of being overtopped because of its comparatively slender limbs. Not a quality horse, but typical of the best type of halfbred.
Height About 15·2 hh.
Colour Black, deep chestnut.
Temperament and characteristics Steady, long-lasting all rounder, and a good, active worker.
Uses A farm and saddle horse. When crossed with Thoroughbred, the stock is improved significantly.
Origin Bulgaria. A breed developed in this century at the State stud near Plieven, from Nonius stallions crossed with Anglo-Arab mares.

East Bulgarian

Appearance Similar to a good sort of Anglo-Arab with a straight profile.
Height Not more than 16 hh.
Colour Chestnut and black.
Temperament and characteristics Steady and good natured with active paces.
Uses Primarily a saddle horse but, as in the case of so many European warm-blood horses, also used in agriculture, and other activities. The breed competes very successfully in all mounted disciplines including racing. It is not so fast as the Thoroughbred and cannot compete on level terms, but it is a willing performer and very temperate.
Origin Bulgaria. An older breed than the Danubian, the type was fixed by the early part of the century and has since been improved by Thoroughbred crosses only. The breed was developed at the Vassil Kolarov State stud and at Stefan Karadja in Dobrudja.

Pleven

Appearance A very Arab-looking horse but bigger than the Arabian and with more substance although still a lightweight, with a wiry physique.
Height About 15·2 hh.
Colour Chestnut.
Temperament and characteristics Spirited, good-natured, intelligent and very active – a natural jumper.
Uses A lightweight riding horse much used for showjumping in its native land but also expected, on occasions, to do some farm work.
Origin The Dimitrov agricultural farm near Pleven, Bulgaria. A very recent breed deriving from Russian Anglo-Arabs and local crossbred and Arabian mares. Later it was crossed with more Arab and with the southern and eastern types of Gidran Arab of Hungary. After 1938, when the breed was considered fixed after barely a quarter of a century, selected English Thoroughbred blood was added.

Greece

Peneia

Appearance Small, sturdy pony of Oriental type.
Height Variable. Not over 14·1 hh.
Colour Nearly all.
Temperament and characteristics Willing, very hardy and frugal.
Uses Farm and pack transport. The stallions are used to breed hinnies.
Origin Peneia, province of Eleia, Peloponnese, Greece. A local breed of Oriental type.

Pindos

Appearance A strong pony of Oriental type.
Height 12–13 hh.
Colour Predominantly dark grey.
Temperament and characteristics A versatile, enduring mountain pony. Very frugal.
Uses Riding and light agriculture. Mares are used to breed mules.
Origin Thessaly, Greece. Ponies were bred in Thessaly in ancient times and were mentioned by the poet, Oppian (*circa* A.D. 211).

Skyros

Appearance A small, light pony, cow-hocked and with poor shoulders. Stunted.
Height Up to 11 hh.
Colour Grey, brown and a 'primitive' sort of dun.
Temperament and characteristics A quiet, frugal pony.
Uses General light farm work and kept on the mainland as children's riding ponies.
Origin Island of Skyros, Greece. Ponies have lived on Skyros since classical times and there is without doubt some resemblance to the Tarpan in their appearance.

Iceland

Iceland Pony

Appearance Stocky, short-bodied pony with short, thick neck and fairly large head. Abundant mane and tail.
Height 12–1 hh.
Colour Usually grey or dun, but also all other colours.
Temperament and characteristics Rugged, intelligent and independent. The toughest of ponies. Noted for its excellent eyesight and a highly developed homing instinct. The ponies move naturally at the *tolt,* a fast, ambling pace.
Uses Light draught and riding, and also kept for meat.
Origin The ponies came to Iceland, with their owners, from Norway in the 800s and were later crossed with ponies brought from the Norse colonies in the Scottish islands, Iceland, and the Isle of Man. There are, therefore, two discernible types, a slightly heavier draught pony and the riding sort. Purists would claim that there are four types. One, the most recognizable, is the Faxafloi which looks something like an Exmoor.

Finland

Finnish Horse

Appearance A small draught type. Very plain but strongly built throughout.
Height No more than 15·2 hh.
Colour Chestnut, bay, brown, black.
Temperament and characteristics Gay, but very quiet to handle. Agile and active with excellent constitution and staying power.
Uses All forms of draught including timber hauling. It is used in trotting races and can be ridden.
Origin Finland. Bred up from native ponies with admixtures of warm and cold blood, performance has always been a priority in what is now Finland's only officially recognized breed. In fact, two types still exist despite merging, the Draught and the lighter General Utility, sometimes called the Finnish Universal.

Norway

Dole—Gudbrandsdal

Appearance Very like the British Dales and the Dutch Friesian, both of which derive from the same basic stock.
Height 14·2—15·2 hh.
Colour Mostly black and brown.
Temperament and characteristics A hardy, powerful horse of even temper.
Uses Primarily bred for agricultural use, it can also be used for riding.
Origin Norway. The Dole seems to have its early origin in the Gudbrandsdal Valley, where a Gudbrandsdal Horse was once bred. The most lasting of the outside crosses that were made in the development of the Dole was the influence of the Thoroughbred Odin imported in 1834. This horse appears in the pedigrees of all modern Doles. Even in the early days of the breed there appear to have been two types, a light and a heavy. Odin and his great-grandson Balder IV (1849) were the principal influences in the former and the stallion Brimen was responsible for the heavier type required to haul the bigger agricultural implements which were being manufactured in the late 1800s. The lighter type is the origin of the Dole Trotter.

Dole Trotter

Appearance Lighter than its relation the Gudbrandsdal and looking more like a Fell.
Height About 15·1 hh.
Colour Brown, black, or bay.
Temperament and characteristics A tough, determined horse, very hard and active. Action notably free at the trot.
Uses Harness and harness racing.
Origin Norway. Developed from the lighter of the Gudbrandsdals and the innate trotting ability realized by the use of trotting stallions. Stallions are tested over 1000 metres (1100 yards), a distance that has to be covered in three minutes for the animals to be accepted in the Stud Book.

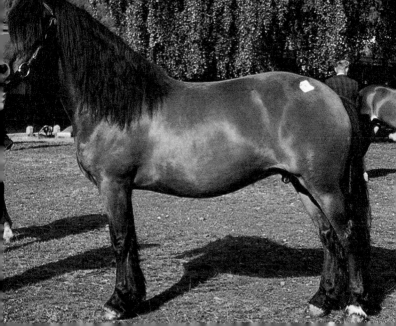

Fjord Pony (Westlands)

Appearance A strong, charming pony, of primitive type with upright mane, but showing refinement in the neat head. Very muscular and compact. No discernible wither. Light feather on the heels of the strong, short legs.
Height 13–14·2 hh.
Colour Dun in all shades with a dorsal stripe. Primitive zebra banding on legs. Mane and tail are silver. The centre of the mane is black.
Temperament and characteristics Self willed and hard working, tough and hardy. Economical feeder and long-lived.
Uses All types of farm work in difficult terrain. Very good in harness.
Origin West Norway. A descendant, recognizably, of the Mongolian Wild Horse. The same sort of pony that has been bred for over 2000 years in northern Europe and was the horse of the Vikings, being used by them in the sport of horse fighting when two horses were matched against each other to the death.

The Fjord is bred all over Scandinavia and has been exported extensively to Denmark, a country with a large population of these delightful ponies.

Northlands

Appearance A pony resembling the Iceland but with a smaller head.
Height About 13 hh.
Colour Usually dark coloured.
Temperament and characteristics Very hardy and frugal and with exceptionally hard legs and feet.
Uses Riding and draught.
Origin Norway. The pony, referred to as a 'horse' in its native land, belongs to the northern pony type derived from Mongolian/Tarpan blood. The northern pony type encompasses the Baltic Pony (Konik) and the Celtic ponies (Shetland, Iceland, Exmoor). The modern Northlands owes much to a selected stallion, Rimfakse, which was nominated as being typical in 1944 and was used considerably to improved the existing stock.

Sweden

Gotland (Skogsruss)

Appearance A small pony showing some primitive character. The feet and legs are hard but otherwise the conformation may leave something to be desired, the back being long and rather weak and the quarters poor.
Height 12–12·2 hh.
Colour Dun, black, brown, chestnut, grey.
Temperament and characteristics A quick-moving, hardy pony that is inclined to be self-willed and uncooperative. The action at walk and trot is acceptable but is otherwise poor. The pony is said to be a good jumper but that is probably a matter of relative comparison.
Uses A trotting racer. As a child's pony for which it would hardly seem an ideal choice. Previously the pony was used for light agricultural work.
Origin Gotland Island, Sweden. The breed is descended from wild ponies, a herd of which still exists, which have inhabited the area from time immemorial and were probably descendants of the Tarpan. About a hundred years ago Oriental blood was introduced.

North Swedish

Appearance A cold-blood heavy horse, small in size and showing primitive origins in the long, large head. Deep in the body, very muscular and with notably good limbs and joints.
Height 15·1–15·3 hh.
Colour Dun, brown, chestnut, black.
Temperament and characteristics Notably active, sound and long-lived. Very willing, and selectively bred for its action and determination in draught work. The breed has a rare immunity to most equine diseases.
Uses General agriculture.
Origin Sweden. Developed from the ancient Scandinavian horse and closely related to the Dole-Gudbrandsdal which was introduced in the last century. A stud book came into being in 1924.

North Swedish Trotter

Appearance A lighter, rangier version of the North Swedish. It is in fact of the same breed.
Height 15·1–15·3 hh.
Colour Black, brown, bay, chestnut, dun.
Temperament and characteristics As the North Swedish but with a fast and active trot in which the stride is exceptionally long.
Uses A trotting racer.
Origin Sweden. The Trotter is of the same breed as the North Swedish, the lighter animals having been selectively interbred. The North Swedish Trotter has the distinction of being the only cold-blood racing trotter in the world. It cannot, of course, be compared in speed with the American Standardbred or similar horses.

Swedish Ardennes

Appearance A compact carthorse similar in appearance to the Belgian Ardennes from which it descends.
Height 15·2–16 hh, although those bred in the hillier country are smaller.
Colour Black, brown, bay, chestnut.
Temperament and characteristics A versatile, active worker with the usual docility of heavy breeds.
Uses Agricultural.
Origin Sweden. The breed originated about a hundred years ago when Belgian Ardennes were crossed with the indigenous North Swedish Horse. A fixed type has now emerged.

Swedish Warm Blood

Appearance A saddle horse of good conformation and usually up to weight. Very deep through the girth, with short, strong limbs.
Height About 16·2 hh.
Colour All solid colours.
Temperament and characteristics A sensible, good-natured horse, strong and sound.
Uses A saddle horse particularly suited to competitive sport, with a talent for dressage.
Origin The stud at Flyinge, Sweden. The horse is the result of a deliberate breeding policy stretching back over 300 years and is the product of an amalgam of bloods. The early horses descended from Oriental, Spanish and Friesian imports but since then use has been made of the best Thoroughbreds, Arabs, Trakehners and Hanoverians.

Denmark

Frederiksborg

Appearance A plain, strong harness horse type with the typical concave face denoting Spanish ancestry. Very powerful shoulders and chest. Good limbs with plenty of bone.
Height Average 15·3 hh.
Colour Usually chestnut.
Temperament and characteristics A willing, tractable horse, active in its paces.
Uses Once a saddle horse used in classical riding and as a military charger, as well as being a carriage horse of the finest class. Today, the Frederiksborg is used as a light draught and harness horse and perhaps increasingly as a general riding horse.
Origin Denmark. The Royal Frederiksborg stud was created in 1562 by King Frederik II and was one of the most notable of its period. The original stock was Spanish (Andalucian) with later importations of Neapolitans. Later, Eastern and British halfbred stallions were introduced. The purpose was to produce active military chargers, and at one time the Frederiksborg was, together with the Andalucian, the foremost riding horse of Europe. Unwise selling of breeding stock resulted in the stud's closure in 1839. The breed, however, was carried on all over Denmark by individual enthusiasts.

Jutland

Appearance A typical massively built, heavy draught horse with a depth of chest exceeding the length of the short, muscular, feathered legs.
Height 15·2–16 hh.
Colour Predominantly chestnut or roan, occasionally bay and black.
Temperament and characteristics A very kind, easily managed horse of great strength and versatility in any form of draught.
Uses Heavy draught.
Origin Jutland Island, Denmark. These famous horses have a history extending over a thousand years and were the warhorses that carried the heavily armoured knights of the 1100s. The modern Jutland stems from an English horse, possibly a Shire but more likely, in view of the predominant chestnut colour, to have been a Suffolk exported in 1860. This was Oppenheim LXII, a dark chestnut with a white blaze. There have also been crosses of Clevelands and the old Yorkshire Coach Horse. The breed, unfortunately, is now in decline.

Knabstrup

Appearance A spotted, lighter edition of the Frederiksborg.
Height About 15·3 hh.
Colour Spotted, on a grey ground.
Temperament and characteristics As the Frederiksborg, but a lighter horse. The outstanding feature is the spotted coat.
Uses Popular as a circus horse.
Origin The breed began in 1808 through the foundation dam, a Spanish spotted mare, Flaebehoppen, put to a Frederiksborg. It is now virtually extinct although spotted horses, resembling the Knabstrup, still exist in Denmark.

Union of Soviet Socialist Republics

Akhal-Teke

Appearance Distinctive and unusual. Long-legged horse with a lean, long body, sloping quarters and low-set tail. Long, thin neck and long, straight face with prominent ears. A narrow, spare, sinewy horse, the mane and tail thin and very fine in texture.
Height 14·2—15·2 hh.
Colour Generally gold with a unique, metallic bloom, but also bay and grey.
Temperament and characteristics A tough, independent horse, often obstinate and bad-tempered, traits which may be the result of rough treatment. Extraordinarily enduring and of very great stamina. Well adapted to the extremes of desert conditions.
Uses A saddle and racehorse of great versatility, its performance in competitive sports being marred only by its uncertain temperament. Even so, Akhal-Tekes have won Olympic medals in dressage.
Origin Turkoman Steppes, USSR. A unique strain of the ancient Turkmene or Turcoman which can be traced back over 2500 years. Bred originally and even today in the central Asian deserts, the best of the present breed comes from the stud at Ashkhabad in Turkestan. Akhal-Tekes with Iomud horses took part in the now famous ride from Ashkhabad to Moscow, a distance of 4275 kilometres (2672 miles), including 360 kilometres (225 miles) of desert which was crossed in three days without the horses being able to drink.

Bashkirsky Pony

Appearance A strong, cobby pony, long in the back but on good limbs. Short, thick neck.
Height About 13·2 hh.
Colour Bay, dun, chestnut.
Temperament and characteristics Steady, hardy, very enduring.
Uses Saddle and sleigh ponies. The mares are milked to make *kumiss*, a potent Asian drink, and are said to produce some 2000 litres (440 gallons) in a lactation period.
Origin Bashkiria, USSR. There are, in fact, two types of pony, the Mountain Bashkir and the Steppe. The former has been improved by crossings with Budyonny and Don Horses, the latter, the harness type ponies, have been crossed with both Trotters and Ardennes stallions.

Budyonny

Appearance A strong, deep-bodied riding horse on short, excellent limbs. Attractive, quality head.

Height 15·2—16 hh.

Colour Predominantly chestnut and often gold, like so many Russian horses, but also bay or grey.

Temperament and characteristics A calm, sensible horse. It has great powers of endurance and stamina, and is a very versatile and consistent performer.

Uses Bred originally as a cavalry horse, the Budyonny is now used for all types of competitive riding including steeplechasing. In this last field it has achieved considerable success in its own country.

Origin Rostov region, USSR. The horse is named after the Russian cavalry general, Marshal Budyonny, the instigator of the breed for cavalry purposes. The basis of the Budyonny is the Don mare crossed with Thoroughbred stallions. From the progeny the best were selected and interbred.

Don

Appearance A 'breedy' type of horse and wiry. A little long on the leg to Western eyes and without the best of pasterns, which are often too upright.

Height 15·1—15·3 hh.

Colour Usually chestnut, occasionally golden, bay or grey.

Temperament and characteristics Equable, tough, hardy and very enduring. A frugal animal able to subsist on poor feeding without losing the capacity to work. Able to live out in harsh climatic conditions. Action is rather short and restricted.

Uses Originally the Cossack cavalry horse, the Don is an all-purpose horse, being used in harness and for riding and long-distance racing events.

Origin The early Dons were crossed with Karabakh and Turkmene horses which were loosed on the Steppes, where the modern Don is still kept in herds and forced to forage for its living. In the 1800s height was given to the Don by outcrossings with Thoroughbreds and the old Strelets Arab.

Iomud

Appearance A similar horse to the Akhal-Teke, but more Arabian in appearance, smaller and less rangy, but still sinewy and strong.
Height 14·2–15 hh.
Colour Most solid colours, but primarily grey with some chestnuts and bays being found.
Temperament and characteristics Possibly because of the presence of Arab blood, the Iomud is of a more kindly disposition than the Akhal-Teke. It is not so fast but has even more stamina. A courageous horse.
Uses A riding horse once used for cavalry. It is particularly esteemed for its ability to race over very long distances. (*See* details of the Askhabad-Moscow ride under Akhal-Teke.)
Origin Central Asia, USSR. Like the Akhal-Teke, the Iomud is a strain of the Turkmene but Arabian influence is noticeable.

Kabardin

Appearance A strong little horse predisposed to slight inward-curving ears. The limbs are strong and the feet good but the quarters are not attractive and the breed frequently exhibits sickle hocks.
Height 14·2–15 hh.
Colour Bay and black.
Temperament and characteristics A calm, steady horse with a remarkable ability for working in mountainous, broken country over rough, narrow tracks. Very sure footed, with a highly developed homing instinct. This is the best of the Russian mountain horses.
Uses A riding horse especially suited to the mountains and for long-distance journeys. It is much used in local sports and is raced. A group of Kabardins in 1935 took part in a trial of 3000 kilometres (1860 miles) over mountainous country and in adverse winter conditions. It was completed in thirty-seven days with every Kabardin finishing.
Origin Mountain areas of the north Caucasus, Russia. The Kabardin has been known and prized as a mountain horse for over 400 years. It derives from the indigenous mountain stock crossed with Arab, Turkmene, and Karabakh.

Karabair

Appearance Arabian in appearance but more stocky and less refined. Wiry with good limbs.
Height About 15·1 hh.
Colour Bay, chestnut, grey.
Temperament and characteristics Steady, tough and enduring but spirited.
Uses Farming work (for heavier types) otherwise a riding and driving type. Karabairs are employed in the fierce and dangerous game of *Kok-par* which in theory involves the carrying of a goat carcass through the opposing goal; in practice, it is a mounted free-for-all with very few noticeable rules.
Origin Uzbekistan, USSR. Uzbekistan has been famed for its horses for over 2000 years but no certain information is available on the origins of this breed. It must be presumed that there is a strong Oriental influence on a mixed background of native and Southern stock. The breed is bred selectively at the Dzhizak stud at Samarkand and in a number of collective farms.

Karabakh

Appearance A strong, handsome pony with an alert head. Very compact and of good conformation. Strong limbs and hard, blue hooves.
Height About 14·1 hh.
Colour Golden dun with the characteristic metallic sheen of so many Russian horses, which is present even when the colour is bay or chestnut.
Temperament and characteristics A good-tempered, energetic little horse with good action; sure footed. A mountain horse.
Uses Mountain riding and in equestrian games like *chavgan* (a form of polo) and *surpanakh* (mounted basketball). They are also raced.
Origin Azerbaijan, USSR. The breed was originally native to the Karabakh mountain lands and has been crossed with Persian horses, the Akhal-Teke and the Arabian. Numbers were sent to the Don steppes in the 1700s and influenced the evolution of the Don Horse. Arabian stallions are still used as outcrosses to effect further improvement at the principal breeding centre, the Akdam stud.

Kazakh

Appearance A Mongolian-type pony.
Height 12·2–13·3 hh.
Colour Bay, chestnut, grey, black and sometimes part-coloured.
Temperament and characteristics A tough steppe pony expected to look after itself in severe weather conditions. A willing pony able to carry weight for long distances without tiring. Some Kazakhs amble as a natural pace.
Uses A riding pony to be used over long distances, a cow pony and a pony for competitive long-distance rides (*baiga*). A good Kazakh can cover 300 kilometres (190 miles) in twenty-four hours. Mares are used for milking and stock is also bred for meat production.
Origin Kazakhstan, USSR. Excavated burial mounds in the region show that ponies identical to the Kazakh lived in this area 1300 years ago. The base is Mongolian but there have been introductions of Don blood.

Kirghiz (Novokirghiz)

Appearance A long-bodied horse on short legs with dense, hard hooves. Neat head, and a very noticeable development of the chest cavity due to the height at which the Novokirghiz is bred, 2000 to 3000 metres (6650 to 9900 feet) above sea-level.
Height 14·2–15 hh.
Colour Usually bay.
Temperament and characteristics Hardy mountain horse able to work at high altitudes. Very tough, active and sure footed. Good tempered.
Uses Mountain riding and pack. Cow pony for use on the high seasonal pastures. Sometimes raced.
Origin Kirghiz, mountains of Tien Shan, USSR. The Novokirghiz evolved from the stunted native Kirghiz crossed with Don and other quality riding breeds some hundred years ago. Selective breeding from the resultant crossbreds began in the 1930s and resulted in the present breed.

Latvian

Appearance A strong harness horse, deep in the body with good limbs which carry some feather on the lower parts.
Height 15·2–16 hh.
Colour Bay, brown, chestnut.
Temperament and characteristics Steady, sensible horse, hard working and versatile with good active movement.
Uses An all-purpose horse for use in draught or under saddle. Much used in agriculture.
Origin Latvia, USSR. Primarily a harness horse, the Latvian is descended from the primitive Forest Horse and has inhabited Latvia from before the time of recorded history. In the 1600s improvement was made by the introduction of the Arab and Thoroughbred and by the use of many of the German saddle and carriage breeds. There was also an early addition of cold blood from the Finnish Draught and the Swedish Ardennes. There seem to be three fairly distinct types of Latvian, the most numerous being the all-purpose animal described. There is, however, a bigger carriage type and a much lighter horse that is a faster harness trotter.

Lithuanian Heavy Draught

Appearance A massive, very short-legged draught horse of medium size. There is a notable tendency to a dipped back and frequently there are sickle hocks.
Height 15–15·3 hh.
Colour Usually chestnut with flaxen mane and tail, but also bay, black, grey and roan.
Temperament and characteristics Docile to the point of dullness. The breed, selectively bred, largely on performance, is very strong and able to pull heavy loads. The action is free and, for a horse of this size, fast.
Uses Agriculture and heavy transport.
Origin Lithuania, USSR. The Lithuanian is the product of the original smaller, but very active Zhmud Horses crossed with Swedish Ardennes. Thereafter, selected progeny from the original cross have been interbred. The breed was registered in 1963.

Lokai

Appearance A tough, wiry horse with a plain, long head. Well-muscled but prone to malformed limbs such as splay feet and sickle hocks. Sparse mane and tail. Sometimes the coat is curled and resembles Astrakhan.
Height About 14·3 hh.
Colour Grey, bay, chestnut, with golden tints in the last two.
Temperament and characteristics Good natured, tough, sure-footed mountain ponies which are rarely shod.
Uses Mountain riding and pack work in high altitudes. Local equestrian sports including the Lokai version of the goat carcass game which is as rough as that played by the Uzbeks.
Origin Tadzhikistan on the western Pamirs, USSR. Bred from the 1500s by the Lokai people, the breed has been crossed with Karabair, Iomud, and Arab horses to effect an improvement.

Orlov Trotter

Appearance A strong, raw-boned horse, long in the back but deep and thick set. Very powerful shoulder, somewhat upright, strong limbs with some feather. A coarse-looking horse but handsome.
Height About 15·3 hh but 17 hh is not unknown.
Colour Grey and black are most usual.
Temperament and characteristics A courageous, persevering horse, bred to trot. Good constitution, a hard horse and long-lived
Uses A racing trotter, and formerly a carriage and troika horse, too.
Origin USSR. The breed was the creation of Count Alexius Grigorievitch Orlov who in 1777 crossed the Arab, Smetanka, with a Dutch mare to produce Polkan. The latter, similarly crossed, sired Bars I in 1784. Bars I, mated with crossbred Arab-Dutch mares, was the foundation of the Orlov Trotter. In the 1800s outside crosses were made to Arabs, Thoroughbreds, Mecklenbergs, and Norfolk Hackney. Trotting is a far more popular sport in Russia than is flat racing, and Orlovs (there are some 30 000) are the horses in principal use though they are not as fast as the Standardbred.

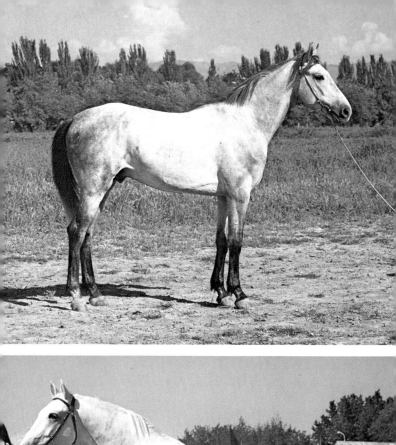

Russian Heavy Draught

Appearance The breed looks more like a heavyweight cob than a true heavy although it is a cold blood.
Height About 14·2 hh.
Colour Usually chestnut in varying shades.
Temperament and characteristics A good-natured worker with great powers of traction and able to work at speed in harness.
Uses General agriculture and heavy harness.
Origin Ukraine, USSR. The breed was founded about a century ago by crossing local mares with Ardennes, Percheron, and Orlov stallions. Thereafter selected progeny were interbred to fix the breed.

Russian Trotter

Appearance A lighter version of the Orlov, but less handsome.
Height About 15·3 hh.
Temperament and characteristics As for a trotter.
Uses A racing trotter.
Origin USSR. The breed evolved during the 1800s and was designed to produce a horse of greater speed than the Orlov. This was achieved by the Orlov/Standardbred cross. The Russian Trotter is, indeed, faster but it does not have the value of the old Orlov as an outcross to cartmares.

Tersky

Appearance Very like a large, purebred Arabian but, because of its size, has lost the Arab's innate refinement.

Height About 15 hh.

Colour Silver grey or even white; skin is pink and gives a rosy tint to the coat.

Temperament and characteristics A kind, lively horse retaining the Arab character and qualities of endurance.

Uses A saddle horse, useful for all-round riding purposes. The Tersky is also raced (against Arabs not Thoroughbreds) and is popular as a circus horse.

Origin Tersk in the northern Caucasus, USSR. The breed came into being to preserve, so far as it was possible, the old Strelets Arabian of the 1800s which had virtually disappeared after World War I. The Strelets was not, in fact, purebred—it was an Anglo-Arab, purebreds having been crossed with Anglos from Orlov and Rastopchin. Two stallions only survived World War II and breeding, following the original policy, was begun again after the cessation of hostilities. Selected crossbreds, conforming to the Strelets type, were then interbred and the Tersk was officially recognized in 1948.

Toric

Appearance A strong cob type of heavy horse, usually with white hooves.

Height 15–15·2 hh.

Colour Usually chestnut or bay.

Temperament and characteristics Steady, hard worker. Like the Latvian and the Lithuanian, it is classed as a warm blood and is able to work fast on the light soils of the area. A durable horse of good constitution.

Uses A harness and working horse.

Origin Estonia, USSR. The foundation of the breed was laid at the Toric stud in Estonia when the Norfolk Roadster, Hatman, was imported in 1894. This horse was mated with the local Estonian mares, known as Kleppers, and was interbred to a large degree. To this base has been added Orlov, East Friesian, Ardennais, Trakehner, Hanoverian, and even Thoroughbred, all in relatively small doses. The result is an active, quick-moving versatile farm horse which is best suited for the agricultural needs of the area.

Viatka

Appearance A pony very like the Polish Konik but larger and of fairly good conformation apart from a tendency towards sickle hocks.
Height 13–14 hh.
Colour Dun, roan or grey. Often there is the primitive dorsal stripe and barred legs.
Temperament and characteristics A very hardy, frugal pony, willing and very strong. The action is short, because of a tendency towards uprightness in the shoulder and the breadth of the chest, but the Viatka is an active mover.
Uses A harness pony used in light agriculture and for pulling troikas.
Origin The Udmurt Republic and Kirov district, USSR. The pony, like so many of the Russian breeds and types, is closely related to the Konik and thus to the Tarpan.

Vladimir

Appearance Like so many of the Russian heavy horses, it is cob-like in appearance but with strong Shire character. The back is long but otherwise the horse is well made and the body set on good, short limbs correctly placed for optimum traction combined with free movement.
Height About 16 hh.
Colour All solid colours.
Temperament and characteristics An energetic, mobile horse of sound constitution and of adequate speed. Tractable and friendly.
Uses Agriculture and heavy draught.
Origin The Ivanovo and Vladimir regions, USSR. The horse is largely of English origin, Clydesdales, Shires, and Suffolks being present in its make-up. The breed was founded at the Gavrilovo-Posadsk stables in 1886, when a mixture of Suffolk Punch, Cleveland, Ardennais, and Percheron blood was introduced to the local mares. In 1910 some Clydesdale and rather more Shire outcrosses were made. Shire crosses continued until 1925 and thereafter the Vladimir relied upon interbreeding of stock to consolidate the type. By 1950 this object had been achieved.

Yakut

Appearance A Mongolian type pony covered with long, thick hair. Deep chested, heavily built and long in the back.

Height About 13 hh.

Colour Greyish or mouse coloured with darker crossing stripes on the shoulders.

Temperament and characteristics Possibly the hardiest of all horses and one of the most remarkable. It exists in winter temperatures of −40 to −45°C (−40 to −50°F), digging its food from under deep snow. In the summer, a very short one, it has to suffer the attacks of blood-sucking insects. It is an enduring and versatile worker.

Uses The Yakut is a riding and pack pony as well as a harness animal. It is used in local equestrian games and it is a source of both milk and meat to its owners.

Origin The coldest areas of the Yakut territory in the Arctic circle, USSR. There are two types of Yakut pony, the larger northern type and a smaller one. The large type is a direct derivative of the Asiatic Wild Horse of Mongolia; the origin of the smaller pony is less clear. It is suggested that it descends from the white Tundra Horse, remains of which have been found in the Yana Valley. (*See* Introduction.)

Zemaituka

Appearance Unprepossessing pony of little conformational merit but strongly built apart from the hocks. A refinement on the basic Asiatic Wild Horse from which it descends.

Height 13–13·3 hh.

Colour Shades of dun with dorsal stripe.

Temperament and characteristics Willing, frugal pony, tough and with stamina. It is said to be able to cover more than 60 kilometres (40 miles) a day on starvation rations.

Uses All general purposes.

Origin Baltic states, USSR. The pony is descended from the Asiatic Wild Horse crossed with the Arab.

Mongolia

The Mongolian Wild Horse (*Equus Przewalskii*)

Appearance A primitive pony type. Large, long-eared head, convex profile. Short, ewe neck, straight shoulders, trailing quarters. Erect mane and sparse tail.

Height 12·1–14 hh.

Colour Dun (between cream and red) with pronounced dorsal stripes, zebra markings on legs.

Temperament and characteristics A wild pony with great powers of endurance and able to withstand the most harsh climatic and environmental conditions. Wary of humans and very fierce in the protection of its young.

Origin Western edges of the Gobi Desert, Mongolia; now preserved in zoos in various parts of the world. The pony, the wild horse of the Mongolian steppes, exists in the same form as in the Ice Age and is one of the basic types from which all horses descend in part. The horse was discovered by the Russian explorer, Colonel N M Przewalski, in 1881 in the area of the Tachin Schah Mountains (literally, the Mountains of the Yellow Horses) which lie on the edge of the Gobi Desert. Whether they exist in the wild state today is doubtful, because they had been hunted almost to the point of extinction several years ago.

Ponies derived from the Wild Horse exist in great numbers throughout the whole of Mongolia, China and Tibet, varying considerably in type because little if any form of selective breeding is practised. These ponies are between 12·3–13 hh in height and are probably little different from those which carried the hordes of Genghis Khan. The ancient horse peoples relied upon their horse herds not only as a means of mobility and transport but as the very staff of life: the herds provided a larder of fresh meat on the hoof, the mares were milked and even the droppings were used to make fires for warmth and cooking. The present peoples of Asia, where they are sufficiently isolated to be unaffected by outside influences, follow much the same pattern of life today.

The ponies have incredible powers of endurance, are fast over short distances and very agile. Like their masters, they can live on the poorest of fare.

Tibet

Tibetan Pony (Nanfan)

Appearance A strong utility pony. It is not notably well formed but the legs and feet are strong and there is more bone than might be expected. Very thick mane and tail.

Height About 12·2 hh.

Colour All colours.

Temperament and characteristics Tough, enduring and frugal. A willing worker and sure footed.

Uses Principally pack, but also used for riding and some agricultural work.

Origin Tibet. A descendant of Chinese and Mongolian ponies and closely allied to the neighbouring Spiti and Bhutia ponies.

India

Bhutia Pony

Appearance A thickset pony, strong, with more bone than is usually evident in Asian horses.

Height 13–13·2 hh.

Colour Usually grey.

Temperament and characteristics Uncertain temper. Sure footed, enduring and frugal.

Uses Principally a pack pony.

Origin The Himalayas, India. A larger pony than that of Spiti, but like the latter closely related to the neighbouring Tibetan pony.

Kathiawari and Marwari (The two breeds are virtually identical.)

Appearance A light, narrow-framed pony often showing typical signs of degeneration. Weak-looking in the quarters and sickle-hocked. The ears, when pricked, curve inwards until they nearly touch at the points. An Arab influence is very evident.

Height About 14—15 hh.

Colour Any, including part-colours.

Temperament and characteristics Generally bad tempered but remarkably tough and enduring. Able to live and work, out of necessity, on very little.

Uses All purposes.

Origin India. The Kathiawari comes from the north-west coast and the Marwari from Rajputana. They are descended from the largely degenerate country-bred stock crossed with Arab horses. The story is that a cargo of Arab horses swam ashore from a shipwreck on the west coast and, running wild, bred with the native stock. The same story is told about so many breeds that we can only wonder at the number of ships carrying consignments of Arabs that managed to be so conveniently wrecked.

Spiti

Appearance A smaller edition of the Bhutia.

Height 12 hh.

Colour Usually grey.

Temperament and characteristics Unpleasant temper but, like the Bhutia, sure footed, tireless and frugal.

Uses Pack ponies on the high mountain paths.

Origin The Himalayas, India. A mountain pony bred principally by the Kanyat, who are traders with neighbouring states. It has a definite connection with the Tibetan Pony.

Assam

Manipur Pony

Appearance A sturdy pony showing evidence of Mongolian and Arab blood.
Height 11–13 hh.
Colour Assorted but no part-colours.
Temperament and characteristics Co-operative, tough, sound and sure footed.
Uses Polo and general purposes.
Origin The hill states of Assam and the Himalayas, Manipur. The breed is by no means pure but the base is the Asiatic Wild Horse with some Arabian outcrosses. The Manipur is regarded as the original polo pony and was used by British planters of the 1850s who took up the local game and thereafter introduced it to the Western world.

Indonesia

Bali Pony

Appearance Primitive type often with upright mane like the Mongolian.
Height 12–13·1 hh.
Colour Primarily dun.
Temperament and characteristics A strong, willing, frugal pony.
Uses Mainly pack but also ridden.
Origin Bali, Indonesia.

Batak

Appearance A superior type of pony in comparison with other Indonesian varieties. The importation of Arab blood has given them a degree of elegance.
Height 12–13 hh.
Colour All.
Temperament and characteristics A docile, good-natured pony but quite spirited. An economical feeder and easily managed.
Uses General, including riding but mainly used as breeding stock.
Origin Island of Sumatra. These ponies form the core of Indonesian breeding. They are carefully selected and bred in proper studs, and Arabs are used to improve the stock, which are then dispensed to other islands to continue the good work. A heavier type of pony, the Gayoe, is bred in the north of Sumatra, but it is not so lively and spirited as the Batak.

Java

Appearance A small, often cow-hocked pony.
Height 12·2 hh.
Colour All.
Temperament and characteristics Willing and seemingly tireless.
Uses The taxi pony of Java; it pulls heavily laden *sados*.
Origin Island of Java.

Sandalwood

Appearance A finer pony than most Indonesians, with pronounced Arab head.
Height 12·1–13·1 hh.
Colour Various.
Temperament and characteristics Spirited and fast. They have fine coats and rarely sweat after exertion.
Uses Bareback racing.
Origin Islands of Sumba and Sumbawa. These are the most valuable of the Indonesian ponies and with sandalwood (from which they get their name) they are Sumba's principal export.

Sumba and Sumbawa (The two are closely related.)

Appearance Primitive.
Height About 12·2 hh.
Colour Dun.
Temperament and characteristics Tough, willing, intelligent ponies.
Uses The ponies compete in dancing competitions with bells attached to the knees. They are ridden bareback by young boys and controlled in the various movements indicated by the beat of the accompanying tom-toms through the lunge line held by their trainer. These ponies also take part in the national sport of lance throwing.
Origin Islands of Sumba and Sumbawa. The Indonesian ponies, resembling the Mongolian in many cases, may have come to the islands with the ancient Chinese. It is interesting to note that, when ridden, the ponies wear bitless bridles of a type very similar to those used in central Asia 4000 years ago. The economy of the Indonesian islands is based largely on the pony.

Burma

Burma Pony (Shan)

Appearance Similar to the Manipur but larger. A plain, unprepossessing pony but active and strong.
Height Variable, but about 13 hh.
Colour Similar to the Manipur.
Temperament and characteristics Often vicious and not very responsive, but very tough and hardy.
Uses Riding and pack ponies. At one time used by the British to play polo.
Origin The Shan states, Burma. An obvious relation of the Manipur.

China

Chinese Pony

Appearance Similar in appearance to the Mongolian. Compact, head of generally poor conformation.
Height Varies according to the area from 12–13 hh.
Colour All, but mainly dun.
Temperament and characteristics Somewhat wild but very hardy and sure footed. Fast over short distances.
Uses Riding generally; also racing.
Origin China. The Chinese Pony is not, in fact, a breed and ponies of this type are to be found all over the east. No controlled breeding with the object of improvement is carried out. The ponies are closely related to the Mongolian Wild Horses which from ancient times have interbred with domestic ponies.

Turkey

Karacabey

Appearance A good-quality horse showing evidence of its Nonius ancestry.
Height 15·3—16·1 hh.
Colour Any solid colour.
Temperament and characteristics A versatile, all-round horse, sensible, willing and enduring.
Uses Saddle horses, cavalry remounts and also used for light agricultural work, draught and pack purposes.
Origin Principally the stud at Karacabey, Turkey. An all-round horse based on native blood crossed with imported Nonius stallions.

Kurdistan Halfbred

Appearance A fine-legged, light-framed pony with a rather poorly developed chest and of no great substance, but wiry.
Height 12·3—14 hh.
Colour Any colours.
Temperament and characteristics A versatile, enduring pony, hardy and tough, and an economical feeder.
Uses Agriculture, light draught, pack and saddle.
Origin Kurdistan, Turkey. A pony native to the area. Efforts have been made to improve the stock by the use of Arabs.

Iran

Arab, Persian

Appearance Corresponding to Arab type.
Height Up to 15·1 hh.
Colour Arabian.
Uses A saddle horse.
Temperament and characteristics Arabian.
Origin Iran. The Persian Arab is claimed by some to be the ancestor of the Desert Arabian, but this must be a very controversial point. Certainly, the Persians were racing horses 2700 years ago and it is claimed that the modern Persian Arabs descend from these. They are in general taller than the desert-bred horse.

Caspian Pony

Appearance A miniature horse with Arab-type head. Fine (or light) of bone and with long cannons.
Height 10–12 hh.
Colour Grey, brown, bay, chestnut.
Temperament and characteristics Tractable, sure footed and reputedly intelligent.
Uses See below.
Origin Elburtz Mountains, Caspian Sea, Iran. The Caspian is thought to be the ancient miniature horse of Mesopotamia (3000 B.C.) but the theory has yet to be proved. It was thought that the Caspian was extinct until some were found in the area, working in carts, in 1965. A stud of Caspians has recently been established in Britain.

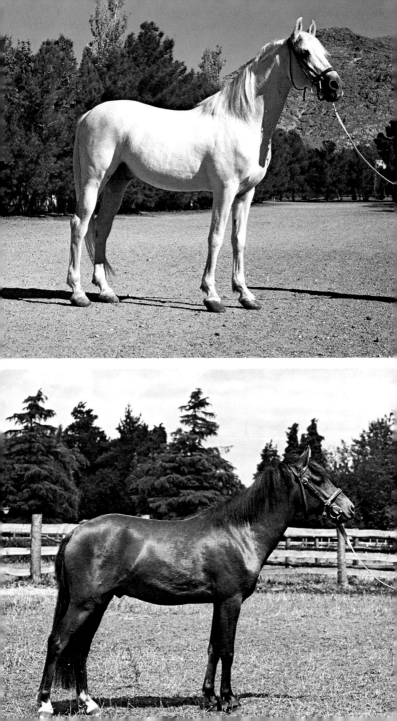

Darashouri (Shirazi)

Appearance A small riding horse with Arabian characteristics.
Height About 15 hh.
Colour Grey, chestnut, bay, brown.
Temperament and characteristic Spirited and intelligent.
Uses A riding horse.
Origin Province of Fars, Iran. It is not possible to define the origin of this horse with any exactitude. The make-up is essentially Oriental and we must assume the presence of Arab blood and guess that there have been crosses with other strains, possibly including the Turkmene.

Jaf

Appearance Very Arabian. A wiry horse.
Height Usually around 15 hh.
Uses A riding horse.
Temperament and characteristics Fiery and courageous but gentle and intelligent. Bred in Kurdistan, it is a plains' horse, not suited to mountainous country.
Origin Kurdistan, Persia. An obviously Oriental horse.

Tchenarani

Appearance An alert Arabian type, very wiry.
Height About 15 hh.
Colour Any solid colour.
Temperament and characteristics Tough and courageous with endurance and stamina.
Uses A cavalry horse.
Origin Northern Iran. The Tchenarani has been bred for over 200 years. In essence it is the product of a Persian Plateau stallion put to a Turkmene mare, this being the favoured cross. It is not usual to breed Tchenarani to Tchenarani because the progeny deteriorate. By European standards the Tchenarani has only a tenuous claim to the distinction of a breed.

Turkoman

Appearance A long-faced, long-eared Oriental of great distinction. Very fine skinned.
Height About 15·2.
Colour Usually golden bay or dun.
Temperament and characteristics Spirited, very fast and with quite exceptional powers of endurance.
Uses A riding horse, but most particularly a racer.
Origin Iran. Descendants of the ancient Turkmene. Their owners, the Turkmen, are passionately fond of racing.

Algeria and Morocco

Barb

Appearance Long head with a straight and sometimes 'ram' profile. Flat shoulders, sloping quarters, and low-set tail.

Height 14–15 hh.

Colour Bay, brown, chestnut, black, grey.

Temperament and characteristics Courageous but with a reputation for bad temper which is probably due to persistent ill usage. Very fast over short distances, enduring over longer ones at a slower pace. Tough and able to exist on short rations.

Uses General riding horse in North Africa. Once used as a cavalry mount.

Origin The north-west of Africa – Morocco, Algeria, and Tunisia. This area, the former Barbary, was noted for its horses 2000 years ago. Historically important as a foundation breed, the Barb was imported into Europe, particularly England, in large numbers in the 1600s. Previously, it had an influence in the evolution of the Andalucian and through that horse on many European breeds. The Barb has been crossed with Arabs but displays little of the Arab conformation or temperament.

Libya

North African Horse (Libyan Barb)

Appearance Plain, with coffin-shaped head, flat shoulders and low-set tail.
Height 14–15 hh.
Colour Bay, brown, chestnut, black, grey.
Temperament and characteristics Excellent constitution, very hardy and active and needing a bare minimum of food.
Uses The horse is used by the military, tribesmen, and for general riding all along the north coast of Africa.
Origin Libya, North Africa. The horse is really the product of the Arab and the Barb and over centuries of warfare and invasions has received blood from many sources.

Nigeria

Nigerian Horse

Appearance The head is plain and the neck poor but the shoulders are often good and strong. Weak quarters but hard legs and feet.
Height 14–14·2 hh.
Colour Any.
Temperament and characteristics A tractable, hardy and willing horse within the limits of its physical conformation.
Uses Light draught, pack and riding.
Origin Nigeria. It seems that horses must have come to this part of the world through the agency of nomadic peoples and perhaps also by deliberate importation. The influence of the Barb horses of the north is quite clearly marked in the Nigerian stock.

Lesotho

Basuto Pony

Appearance Small, thick-set pony, long in the back but standing on short legs and very hard feet.

Height About 14·2 hh.

Colour Chestnut, bay, brown, grey.

Temperament and characteristics Hardy and very enduring, willing and up to weight. Versatile.

Uses Riding and pack. Once used for both polo and racing.

Origin Lesotho, southern Africa. The Basuto is not indigenous. It is descended from Arabs and Barbs imported from Java in 1653. These horses became the Cape Horse, which had something to do with the development of the Australian Waler. The Cape Horse crossed over into Lesotho (formerly Basutoland) in the first half of the 1800s and deteriorated into what we now know as the Basuto Pony.

Australia

Australian Pony

Appearance A compact, strong, cobby sort with marked Welsh character.
Height 12–14 hh.
Colour Assorted, with grey being the most common. No part-colours.
Temperament and characteristics Equable but gay, hardy and sound, with good, free movement.
Uses Children's riding pony.
Origin Australia. Bred from imported British native ponies, mainly Welsh Mountain mixed with a little of the other imported pony bloods together with Arab and Thoroughbred. It is not known outside Australia.

Brumby

Appearance Varied. Basically, a degenerate scrub horse.
Colour Assorted.
Height Very varied up to 15 hh.
Temperament and characteristics Wild, difficult to approach and not amenable to training.
Uses Wild stock that at times assumes pest proportions and has to be culled by shooting and trapping.
Origin Australia. Brumbies (an adaption of the aboriginal word meaning wild) are descendants of domestic horses turned loose on the ranges during the gold rush of the mid-1800s. Australia has no indigenous horse.

Waler

Appearance The best have Thoroughbred characteristics.
Height 16 hh average.
Colour As in the Thoroughbred.
Temperament and characteristics Kind and sensible, more hardy and enduring than the Thoroughbred and with more stamina.
Uses General saddle horses, police and cavalry mounts.
Origin New South Wales, Australia. Early ancestors were Spanish horses brought from the Cape of Good Hope in 1798 to which were added later imports from England. By 1850, when Walers were sent as remounts for the Indian cavalry regiments, the breed had been much improved by the liberal use of Arabs and Thoroughbreds, to the extent that it resembled good class Anglo-Arab.

Canada

Canadian Cutting Horse

Appearance Almost identical to the American Quarter Horse from which it was developed.
Height 15·2—16·1 hh.
Colour Almost any.
Temperament and characteristics Intelligent and adaptable with an inbred ability to work cattle.
Uses A cattle horse, highly developed in Canada for competition events.
Origin Canada. The Cutting Horse is the Canadian equivalent of the Quarter Horse and is the most prominent of today's Canadian horses.

Sable Island Pony

Appearance Small, wiry animals of generally moderate conformation but with occasional good specimens.
Height About 14 hh.
Colour Chestnut, bay, brown, black and grey.
Temperament and characteristics Relatively docile if caught up and schooled early enough. Very hardy by reason of their environment (see below).
Uses Saddle and light draught.
Origin Sable Island (a sandbank with little natural vegetation) off Nova Scotia, Canada. Some 300 ponies exist on the island, descendants of 1700s New England stock (predominantly French).

United States of America

Albino

Appearance Variable but usually (in the United States) a lightweight horse of Oriental character.
Height Any.
Colour Pure white with pink skin; eyes usually pale-blue but sometimes dark.
Temperament and characteristics The Albino is claimed to be very gentle and intelligent but to horsemen the absence of pigmentation denotes a weakness of constitution. So far, no Albino has ever made its mark in any equestrian sphere. The skin is sensitive to the sun and weather and the eyes are weak and subject to defect.
Uses Suitable for circuses and parades.
Origin Albinos may occur anywhere, but in the United States they are bred deliberately and have a governing body, the American Albino Horse Club. It is arguable whether the Albino is, in fact, a breed. The claim to breed status is based on the Albino's ability to breed true to colour, but that is only one criterion for a breed and the least important. Albinos have, however, been bred in North America since just after the turn of the century, all claiming descent from one foundation sire, Old King, which may have been of Arab/Morgan origin.

American Saddle Horse

Appearance A horse of enormous presence if decidedly artificial in appearance. The head, small and very elegant, is set on to a long, muscled neck, which runs into powerful shoulders. The legs are graceful and muscular; the feet are grown long in front. The coat is very fine and the tail is nicked and, therefore, forced into a high carriage. When standing with hindlegs outstretched it resembles the Hackney Horse.

Height 15–16 hh.

Colour Bay, brown, black and chestnut preferably with white markings.

Temperament and characteristics Spirited, courageous and capable of a most spectacular, extravagant, elevated action.

Uses A show-ring horse displayed in one of three ways: 1, as a harness horse shown at walk and a brilliant, controlled park trot; 2, as a three-gaited saddler shown under saddle at walk, trot, and canter; and 3, (at the breed's best) as a five-gaited saddler. In addition to the three basic paces, the horse performs the slow-gait and the crowd-rousing rack.

Origin Originally Kentucky, USA. Initially, the Kentucky Saddler was bred as a practical, if luxurious, means of overseeing the southern plantations. The foundation sires were the Thoroughbred, Denmark, (1839), and his son, Denmark 61, out of a pacing mare. Denmark, with a background of Norfolk Roadster, appears in the pedigrees of Hackney Horses which may account for the appearance and movement of the Saddler. There are also elements of the extinct Narragansett and Canadian Pacers (the latter a pacing horse of French origin) and of Morgan blood in the make-up of the breed.

American Quarter Horse

Appearance A very compact, chunky horse with massive and muscular quarters. Very well proportioned.

Height About 15·2 hh.

Colour Often chestnut, but any solid colour.

Temperament and characteristics Intelligent, tractable, very agile and athletic. Very fast over short distances.

Uses An all-round pleasure horse, the supreme cow pony and a racehorse over short distances.

Origin The United States. The Quarter Horse is the first all-American breed and arguably the world's most popular horse. There are 800 000 registered in the United States and forty-two other countries. The breed began in the Carolinas and Virginia, where English colonists crossed Spanish mares with imported stallions of the blood. The process was also reversed, English mares being put to Spanish stallions. The progeny were used in harness and under saddle and were raced over rough tracks cut out of the undergrowth, or even down the length of the village street. The distances were short and so demanded enormous acceleration from a standing start. In time the distance was fixed at 400 metres ($\frac{1}{4}$ mile) and so the name Quarter Horse came about. The development of the faster Thoroughbred and the introduction of oval tracks eclipsed the Quarter Horse as a racer and the breed moved with the migration to the west to become a cattle horse.

Recently, short-distance racing has been revived in the United States and the Quarter Horse now races for one of the world's biggest prizes, the $600 000 All-American Futurity Stakes.

American Shetland

Appearance A very refined pony with pronounced Hackney character plus an Oriental overlay.

Height Not over 11·2 hh, average 10·2 hh.

Colour Various.

Temperament and characteristics Intelligent and spirited, the American Shetland, despite its 'new look', is said to retain its native hardiness and constitution, but this is arguable. The action, quite unlike that of the Shetland, is high and extravagant like the Hackney.

Uses Primarily as a harness pony for the show-ring but also as a racing trotter and under saddle.

Origin The United States. The American Shetland has come about by the careful selection of the finer type of Island Shetlands mainly crossed with Hackney Ponies and with some infusion of Arab and small Thoroughbred. The result is a fine, lighweight pony that bears little if any resemblance to the Shetland. The use of artificial trotting aids to encourage the gait and the practice of tail-nicking makes their native origin still less recognizable.

American Standardbred

Appearance A short-legged horse, long in the body, and usually with a plain head. Exceptionally powerful quarters. Feet very hard. A muscular horse not so refined as the Thoroughbred. Very deep through the girth.

Height About 15·2 hh.

Colour All solid colours.

Temperament and characteristics A determined, courageous horse with exceptionally free and straight action at the trot (a necessity if the limbs are not to be damaged at the high speed which this breed can attain). Great stamina.

Uses A superlative racing trotter, moving usually with the pacing action.

Origin The United States. The Standardbred evolved from an admixture of Narragansett and Canadian Pacers and the Morgan Horse. The most important development in the breed, however, was the Thoroughbred influence which began through Messenger (1780), a descendant of the Darley Arabian, the line being through his sire, Mambrino, to Engineer, Sampson, Blaze, and Flying Childers.

The foundation sire of the modern Standardbred is accepted as being Hambletonian 10 or Rysdy's Hambletonian (1849), who descended from Messenger. 90 per cent of all Standardbreds descend from him. Between 1851 and 1875 this remarkable stallion sired no less than 1335 off-spring. The name Standardbred derives from the early practice of establishing a speed standard as a requirement for entry in the Trotting Register of 2·30 minutes for conventional trotters over 1·6 kilometres (1 mile) and 2·25 minutes for pacers. Today, the standard has been reduced to 2·20 minutes.

Appaloosa

Appearance A compact horse with well-developed quarters and second thighs. Tail and mane sparse and short. White sclera round the eyes. The skin of the nose, lips and genitals is always a mottled pink and the hooves are marked with vertical black-and-white stripes.

Height 14·2–15·2 hh.

Colour Spotted, usually on a roan ground. There are six patterns of Appaloosa colouring: leopard, snowflake, marble, frost, spotted blanket, and white blanket. Appaloosas are generally associated with spots but it is possible for an animal to be a whole-flecked roan colour.

Temperament and characteristics An exceptionally tractable, sensible horse, agile, athletic and very versatile. Many Appaloosas are good fast jumpers. They also have considerable endurance and stamina.

Uses An excellent, easily kept, all-round riding horse, and a striking parade horse and circus performer.

Origin Palouse Valley, Idaho, United States. Most American breeds were developed by European settlers, but the Appaloosa was developed by the Nez Perce Indians from Spanish horses brought to the Americas by the *conquistadores* in the 1500s. The breeding of spotted horses is very ancient and horses of similar markings can be seen in early Chinese and Persian art. There is ample evidence to show that there was once a spotted strain of Spanish horse, a strain which may have gone into Spain from central Asia. Riddinger's pictures of the Spanish School at Vienna, painted in the 1700s, show a number of spotted Andalucians. The spotted Andalucian strain has long since disappeared but on the other side of the world it is preserved in the colourful Appaloosa. The name Appaloosa is a corruption of Palouse, or Palousy.

The breed went into decline after the breaking up of the Indian tribal lands and between the two World Wars, but over about the past thirty years the Appaloosa has experienced a renewed popularity and his now numbered among the United States' top five breeds, together with the Quarter Horse, the Thoroughbred, the Standardbred, and the American Shetland.

Chincoteague and Assateague Ponies

Appearance A stunted horse of no fixed type and without pony characteristics.
Height About 12 hh.
Colour Any; many are part-coloured.
Temperament and characteristics Generally are stubborn and ill-tempered.
Uses With careful training these ponies might be suitable for children if there was no better material available. They can be used in harness also.
Origin The Chincoteague and Assateague Islands, off the coast of Virginia and Maryland, United States. These 'ponies' are reputedly descended from a cargo of Moorish horses shipwrecked in early colonial times. Assateague is uninhabited and it is possible that the ponies could have survived there undetected for a period of time. Each year, on the last Thursday and Friday of July, the ponies are swum across the narrow channel separating Assateague from Chincoteague and are sold by auction.

Missouri Fox Trotter

Appearance A strong saddle horse, compact and up to weight. The head is attractive and alert tapering to a small muzzle.
Height 14–16 hh.
Colour All colours including part-colours.
Temperament and characteristics A well-mannered saddle horse distinguished by its peculiar broken gait which is nonetheless a comfortable one. The horse walks briskly with the forefeet and trots behind, the hind feet covering the imprint of the forefeet. The head nods in time with the beat and the horse can travel at a speed between 8 and 16 kilometres an hour (5 and 10 miles an hour). The gait is known as a fox trot.
Uses A utility horse used to transport its owners about the hills. Nowadays there are show classes for this little-known trotter.
Origin The Ozark hills of Missouri and Arkansas, United States. The first European settlers in the area brought with them Thoroughbred, Arab, and Morgan horses and from these developed particular lines, the most famous being the Brimmers. By selective breeding, a type became fixed with the characteristic movement. In recent years crosses have been made to the Saddle Horse and the Tennessee Walking Horse.

Morgan

Appearance A powerful little horse with a strong, crested neck and a nicely proportioned, neat head. Great strength in the shoulder and loins and with good, hard legs and feet.

Height 14·2–15·2 hh.

Colour Bay, black, brown, chestnut.

Temperament and characteristics Intelligent and easily handled. Clean, free action. Very versatile and willing. Tough, hardy, with limitless endurance and stamina. Extreme physical strength.

Uses An all-round pleasure horse, a show horse in harness and under saddle, a utility harness horse and weight-pulling competition horse.

Origin The United States. The prowess of the foundation stallion, Justin Morgan, is part of American folklore. Sired either by a Welsh cob or by a Thoroughbred, True Briton, and with an Arab strain, this horse is supposed to have been foaled at West Springfield, Massachussetts, and took his name from his second owner, who bought him in about 1795. Standing a modest 14 hh and weighing only 360 kilograms (800 pounds), Justin Morgan excelled equally as a workhorse and racer, at weight-pulling contests and as a potent and prolific sire. His statue is at the University of Vermont's Morgan Horse Farm. Today's Morgans vary in height but are otherwise consistent in type. They look more refined than their ancestor but are equally versatile.

Mustang

Appearance A scrub type of lightweight horse varying in conformation.

Height 14–15 hh.

Colour All.

Temperament and characteristics Wary, independent and intractable.

Uses Once a utility horse on the ranges, later used for rodeos, but now in serious decline, although it is protected in the free state.

Origin The United States. The Mustang descends from the horses brought by the *conquistadores* which either escaped or were turned loose, migrating through Mexico to the United States. They formed the basis for many breeds and were the ponies used by the Indian tribes.

Palomino

Appearance Varied. Palomino is a colour type and not accepted as a breed even in the United States.

Height Palomino colouring can be found in horses and ponies of every size but in the United States the Association of Palomino Horse Breeders, which is trying to establish the Palomino as a breed, recognizes horses of good saddle type between 14·2–15·3 hh.

Colour Gold, the colour of a newly minted coin, with white mane and tail containing not more than 15 per cent dark hairs.

Temperament and characteristics Variable for the reasons given.

Uses A saddle horse, much prized as a parade horse.

Origin Bred all over the world but in greater numbers in the United States than elsewhere. The Palomino, or Ysabella, so-called after the Spanish queen of that name, has been known and esteemed for its colour from ancient times. Its introduction to America belongs to the early Spanish horses.

Pinto

Appearance A general-purpose riding horse of no specific conformation.

Height Variable.

Colour Piebald or skewbald. *Overo* (piebald) is a recessive gene predominating in South America, while *tobiano* (skewbald), a dominant gene, is more pronounced in North America.

Temperament and characteristics Variable.

Uses General riding horse.

Origin Coloured horses appear all over the world but only in the United States are they recognized as a breed under the Pinto Horse Association, founded in 1956. The word pinto comes from the Spanish, meaning painted.

Pony of the Americas

Appearance A miniature Appaloosa.
Height 11·2–13 hh.
Colour Appaloosa colouring.
Temperament and characteristics As for the Appaloosa.
Uses A young people's all-round pony used in all types of riding competition in both eastern and western styles.
Origin The United States. The breed was founded as recently as 1956 by Mr Leslie Boomhower of Iowa. He crossed a Shetland stallion with an Appaloosa mare to create a miniature spotted horse. To qualify for registration in the stud book animals have to fulfil stringent conformational specifications as well as having the traditional markings. Over 1300 ponies are now registered.

Tennessee Walker

Appearance Neat, straight-profiled head set on a long, powerful neck. Well-set withers and shoulders, square barrel. Powerful limbs. Tail frequently set artificially high.
Height 15–15·2 hh.
Colour Black, white, bay, chestnut.
Temperament and characteristics The Tennessee Walker is claimed to be the most naturally amiable and good tempered of all breeds and to be the most comfortable horse in the world. The feature of the breed is the pace, a four-beat glide, half walk and half run, that transmits scarcely any movement to the rider. The horse is so steady and reliable that it can be ridden by a nervous beginner without qualms.
Uses A pleasure horse.
Origin Tennessee, United States. The Walker, once known as the Turnrow for its ability to inspect crops row by row without damaging the plants, evolved as a stylish mount for gentlemen spending long hours in the saddle inspecting their properties. Numerous breeds have been concerned with the Tennessee Walker: the old Naragansett and Canadian Pacers, Arabs, Thoroughbreds and Morgans but a Standardbred stallion is designated as the foundation sire. This horse was Black Allan, an animal quite useless for racing because of his preference for the peculiar walking pace which has become a unique feature of his descendants. Tennessee Walkers are very popular and there are some 50 000 of them in the United States. An annual Walking Horse Show is held at Shelbyville, Tennessee.

Mexico

Galiceno Pony

Appearance A lightly-built pony that still manages to be compact in build. A fine head, shoulders tending to be upright and the chest narrow. Good feet.
Height 12–13·2 hh.
Colour Bay, black, dun, grey, chestnut.
Temperament and characteristics An intelligent, versatile pony. It has the peculiarity of a natural, fast, running walk.
Uses A western competition pony and ranch pony, also able to be used in harness.
Origin Mexico, from whence it has spread into the United States. The ponies are descended from the Spanish horses which re-instated the horse in the Americas in the 1500s, coming to the New World from Hispaniola. Their ancestors are most likely to have been the Garrano and Sorraia ponies of Portugal and Spain.

Native Mexican

Appearance A small, wiry saddle horse of varying type. Hard bone and good feet.
Height About 15 hh.
Colour Any colour.
Temperament and characteristics A quick, agile and responsive horse, very versatile and tough.
Uses Ranch work and sometimes used in the Mexican bullrings.
Origin Like most American horses it descends from those brought by the Spanish *conquistadores*. It must, therefore, contain the blood of many breeds, including the Andalucian, Arab, and Criollo as well as that of the wild Mustang, itself deriving from Spanish stock.

Puerto Rico

Paso Fino

Appearance A small, strong, impressive horse. Andalucian in character.
Height About 14·3 hh.
Colour All colours.
Temperament and characteristics Gay, intelligent and easily managed. The most arresting feature of the Paso Fino is the three natural, lateral, four-beat gaits: Paso Fino, a slow, collected and highly elevated display gait; Paso Corto, the normal easy travelling gait; and Paso Largo, the extended gait, in which speeds of up to 26 kilometres an hour (16 miles an hour) can be reached with no discomfort to the rider.
Uses A specialist riding horse.
Origin Puerto Rico, but also bred in Colombia, Peru, and the United States. The Paso Fino seems to be an exact derivation of the Spanish horse of the 1500s and to have retained gaits which were once common in Europe and for which particular Spanish strains were noted. The gaits in the Paso Fino have doubtless been retained by the most selective breeding.

Peru

Costeño (Criollo)
See Argentina, Criollo

Peruvian Paso (Peruvian Stepping Horse)
See Algeria and Morocco, Barb

Brazil

Crioulo
See Argentina, Criollo

Mangalarga

Appearance A fairly light-framed horse with a long, Spanish-type head, good withers and shoulder. Low-set tail on powerful quarters, rather long legs but with good bone.
Height About 15 hh but as much as 15·3 hh.
Colour Bay, chestnut, roan, grey.
Temperament and characteristics Willing, very tough, and with exceptional stamina and endurance. Occasionally Mangalargas show a peculiar gait, between trot and canter, called *marcha*.
Uses General riding horse.
Origin Brazil. The breed is about 100 years old and based on Andalucian and Altér Real stallions crossed with Crioulo mares. The founding stallion is recognized as having been Sublime, of Minas Gerais. The breed is also known as the Junqueira. The Campolino is an improved breed based on the Mangalarga and instigated by Cassiano Campolino in 1840. These are heavier, shorter-legged horses and made good cavalry mounts.

Argentina

Criollo

Appearance Compact, large chested and very muscular, particularly in the neck. Well-rounded body and quarters, flat, broad face. Variations are bred throughout South America.
Height 13·3–15 hh.
Colour Dun, roan, chestnut, grey, black, bay, and sometimes Palomino.
Temperament and characteristics Tractable, sound and tough. Exceptional powers of endurance and stamina and an ability to carry weight.
Uses Stock horses and general riding mounts.
Origin Basically in the original Spanish stock imported by the *conquistadores* in the 1500s – a mixture of Barb, Andalucian, and Arab. The Criollo varies a little from one country (and environment) to another. In Brazil it is the Crioulo; in Peru, the Costeño and Morochuco; in Chile the Caballo Chilero; and in Venezuela the Lhanero. Despite differences in height and to a lesser extent in conformation, all these horses are of common origin.

Falabella

Appearance A miniature horse.
Height Under 7 hh.
Colour Any, but modern trends are towards spotted coat patterns.
Temperament and characteristics Very friendly. Continual down-grading for size has resulted in a loss of strength and vigour.
Uses Popular as a pet and occasionally used in North America as a harness pony. Not suitable for riding.
Origin Developed by the Falabella family on their ranch near Buenos Aires from a small Thoroughbred crossed with the smallest Shetlands and thereafter inbred. The 'breed' is about a hundred years old but no precise records exist. It is bred outside the Argentine and there is even a stud in England.

The Importance of Conformation

In simple terms 'conformation' describes the way a horse is put together – its 'make and shape' – and it is much concerned with the proportion of the individual parts to each other. The bone structure is the governing factor in the overall conformation of an animal and dictates the proportions of the structure's component points.

A well-made, proportionate horse will perform his work more efficiently, over a longer period of time, with less risk of strain and stress, than will one of faulty conformation, because no one part of the structure will be exposed to excessive and possibly disabling wear. Furthermore, good proportions result in a good balance of the whole structure and in better, more economical action of the limbs. The conformation of a horse also has a bearing upon its temperament. Badly-made horses, compelled to perform work which, because of the defects in their overall structure, is difficult for them and causes discomfort will naturally enough become bad-tempered.

What constitutes good conformation, however, will alter according to the purpose for which the animal is required. The conformation most suited to a hunter or cross-country horse will not, for instance, do for a carriage horse; any more than the conformation of a carriage horse will fit him to haul a heavy brewers' dray. The thick-set, stocky build of the Lipizzaner is well suited to the disciplines of the *Haute Ecole,* but would be useless on a race course, whereas the 'greyhound' build of the racehorse is ideal for the purpose of speed but not much good for that of draught work.

At the extremes of conformation there are the long, slender bones of the racehorse, with similarly long muscle formations; and the heavy draught horse's thick, short bones and blocks of heavy muscle. The latter conformation gives great power but little speed; the conformation of the racehorse, on the other hand, is conducive to the greatest possible speed in movement. Between these extremes there is a multitude of variations. To produce horses which will fulfil their purpose more efficiently, breeders will introduce out-crosses, increasing the power factor by the use of a heavier type of mare or stallion — as might be the case in big continental show jumpers — or bringing in refinement, leading to freer, more active movement by using horses built primarily for speed.

For these and other reasons the task of defining 'correct' conformation, other than at the extremes of the spectrum, is very difficult, and not made easier by differences of personal opinion and national taste. Despite these divergences most breed societies are unanimous about what constitutes the best conformation of a riding horse, for instance. However, the differences in the actual animals are still very noticeable. What represents 'a good shoulder' to one judge may not be immediately recognizable as such by another. Nonetheless an examination of the generally-accepted points of agreement is valuable in the understanding of 'conformation appropriate to a purpose'.

All authorities agree on the need for good proportions. Over-large heads, for instance, set on weak necks, disturb the balance by placing too much weight on the forehand. Similarly, over-long backs are an obvious indication of weakness in a structure that despite all human efforts is still far from ideal for carrying weight. An extra short back, on the other hand, may indicate strength, but not speed. The more glaring faults of conformation are easily seen by viewing a horse from the side but thereafter an assessment is made by studying the individual parts: the head, the neck, withers and shoulders, forelegs including the feet, chest, girth, back, loins, quarters and hindlegs. The action of a horse, other things being equal, almost always derives entirely from the conformation, faulty conformation producing bad action and vice-versa.

In the head of a horse, as in the whole appearance, a distinct refinement or 'quality' is desirable, typified in a clean-cut, lean head, with the veins showing clearly beneath the thin skin. The opposite to a quality head is a 'common' one, found in the heavy, cold-blood horses and in those cross-breds influenced by them. The Arab head is, indeed, the epitome of 'quality'. The Thoroughbred head, although dissimilar, can be said to show its own distinctive 'quality'. An Arab head displays a distinctly 'dished' (concave) profile, the muzzle tapering gracefully to wide, flared nostrils. The eye is of great size and beauty and the ears small, alert and mobile. The Thoroughbred head is not dished, or so wide, but should not present a 'Roman' (convex) profile, which denotes plebeian ancestry. In fact the Andalucian and its derivatives have Roman noses, but in their case the profile is more often described as 'hawk-like'.

A large, calm eye is associated with a generous nature, while a small sunken 'pig' eye is held to denote bad temper. The eyes, separated by a *fairly* wide forehead, need to be placed pretty well to the front for good forward vision. Common-bred horses (the term used to describe anything outside the pure or near pure bloods, even the majestic 'heavies') have their eyes on the side of the head.

In a quality horse the ears are neat and mobile and not thickly covered in hair. Ears, indeed, are of great value to the horseman, since they signal the horse's state of mind and his intentions. Laid-back ears are a sign of annoyance, temper, or even impending mischief. When the ears are cocked forward the horse's attention has usually been attracted. Ears which flick backwards and forwards mean that a horse is happily giving his rider full attention and is concerned to catch immediately the slightest hint of his wishes. Common ears, being less mobile and expressive, are not so well fitted to communicate.

Points of the horse

1, Poll; 2, Ear; 3, Forelock; 4, Forehead; 5, Eye; 6, Cheek. 7, Nose; 8, Jaw; 9, Nostril; 10, Muzzle; 11, Chin; 12, Chin groove; 13, Jowl; 14, Throat; 15, Shoulder; 16, Jugular groove; 17, Windpipe; 18, Point of shoulder; 19, Shoulder; 20, Breast; 21, Forearm; 22, Knee; 23, Fore cannon; 24, Pastern; 25, Coronet; 26, Hoof; 27, Crest; 28, Mane; 29, Neck; 30, Withers; 31, Ribs; 32, Back; 33, Point of hip; 34, Loins; 35, Point of croup; 36, Flank; 37, Croup;

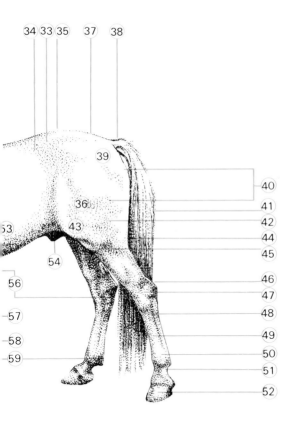

38, Dock; 39, Hind quarters; 40, Buttock; 41, Tail; 42, Thigh; 43, Stifle joint; 44, Hamstring; 45, Second thigh or gaskin; 46, Point of hock; 47, Hock; 48, Flexor tendons; 49, Hind cannon; 50, Fetlock joint; 51, Hallow of heel; 52, Wall of foot; 53, Belly; 54, Prepuce or sheath; 55, Elbow; 56 Chestnuts; 57, Flexor tendons; 58, Back tendons; 59, Ergots; 60, Girth.

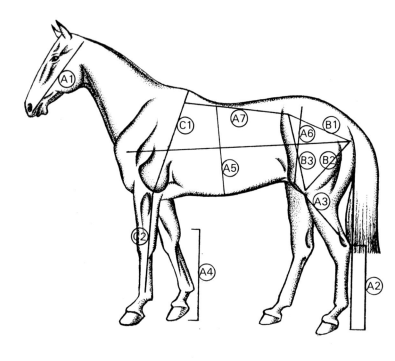

Fig. 3 The proportions of perfect conformation
A1, the length of the head, is equal to the following measurements: **A2**, point of hock to the ground; **A3**, point of hock to fold of stifle; **A4**, chestnut to base of foot; **A5**, depth of girth; **A6**, fold of stifle to croup; **A7**, point of hip to posterior angle of scapula.

B1, length from seat bone to point of hip, equals **B2**, seat bone to stifle and **B3**, stifle to point of hip.

C1, length from wither to elbow, equals **C2**, length from elbow to fetlock.

A vertical line dropped from the seat bone meets the point of the hock and is parallel with the back of the cannon bone.

Length from seat bone to point of shoulder equals about $2\frac{1}{2}$ times the length of the head.

In a horse that is expected to work at speed and often under stress, the nostrils must be large and wide to permit maximum possible air intake. The nostrils are the horse's sole means of breathing, since he cannot use his mouth for this purpose. Ideally, the head should join a graceful, fairly arched neck at an angle of between 90 and 100 degrees. Should the angle be more acute, the horse is more likely to become overbent when ridden and so more subject to unsoundness in the wind. A less acute angle makes correct bridling virtually impossible. The head and neck act as a weighted pendulum to govern the balance of the horse and the consequent distribution of the weight. Heavy heads on weak necks predispose towards weight carried on the forehand, but heavy heads are acceptable if they are set well on to short, thick and therefore strong necks, as is the case with a weight-carrier and, in particular, with some of the German breeds. It is essential that a riding horse should have ample width between the lower jawbones, where the head joins on to the neck. Without this width the horse cannot flex to the bit from the poll. The same is true of horses that are exceptionally thick through the jowl. The neck, withers and shoulders of the horse are all inter-dependent to a very large degree and a deficiency in one will have its effect on the other two.

The neck of a riding horse must be long, but not too much so, and strong enough to support the head. Equally important is the way that the neck joins the shoulders. Ideally, the neck has to be broad at its base blending without interruption into the shoulders. As long as the head is in proportion this arrangement will allow for high carriage of head and neck, giving better balance and control. Necks to be avoided include the 'swan-neck' and the 'ewe-neck'. Both make bridling and control difficult. In the 'swan-neck' there is a pronounced upward curve in the upper third, so that the head joins the neck in an almost vertical line; in a 'ewe-neck' the neck is concave along the top and there is a pronounced muscular develop-ment on the underside. Short necks are, of course, found in some riding horses. As long as the shoulder is reasonably sloping this is no disadvantage when speed is not a factor. Longish necks, with fine heads, are the prerequisite for a good length of stride and speed.

The wither in a riding horse needs to be prominent if the upper part of the shoulder, or scapula, is to be sufficiently long and laid back to allow free movement of the forelegs. But very high withers, although often associated with comfortable rides, are usually weak. Low, flat withers are almost always associated with straight shoulders, which cause the horse to go with a short, bent-knee stride. Arabian horses, however, often have rather flat withers but they are an exception and might be said to make their own rules of conformation.

Good or bad shoulders and what constitutes either are a con-tinuing source of conversation and controversy for horse people.

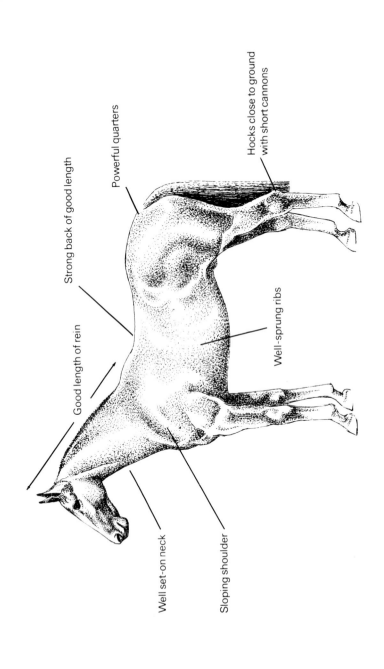

Strong back of good length

Powerful quarters

Hocks close to ground with short cannons

Good length of rein

Well-sprung ribs

Well set-on neck

Sloping shoulder

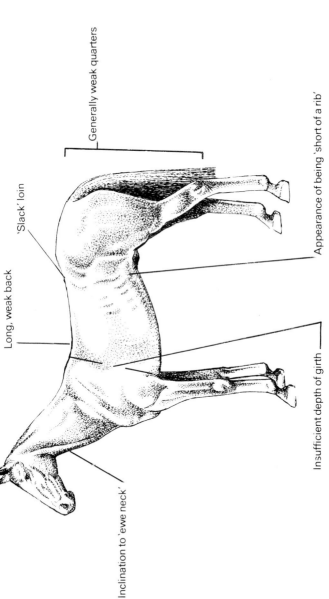

Generally weak quarters

'Slack' loin

Long, weak back

Inclination to 'ewe neck'

Appearance of being 'short of a rib'

Insufficient depth of girth

Fig. 4 A side view of a horse reveals the more obvious strengths and weaknesses of conformation. (above) Average to good. (below) Poor.

Fig. 5 The head and neck are an important guide to the 'quality' of a horse. (above) Good hunter head set on long, graceful neck. (below) Common head set on weak, ill-formed neck.

Most of them agree that the shoulder of the riding horse should be long and well-sloped for the ride to be comfortable, the stride long and economical and if the concussion sustained by the fore-legs is to be minimized. However, while a sloping scapula combined with a humerus which is shaped and positioned so as to bring the forearm well forward (rather than back under the body) is ideal when speed and extension are the criteria, they do not occur in *all* riding horses. They would not, for instance, be appreciated in the Andalucian and his relatives, or in the American Saddle Horse, the park Morgan and many others. A feature of these breeds is the high, ultra-extravagant action in front which English and Irish horse people would find wasteful and ineffectual. The fact that the make and shape of these breeds restricts their capacity to gallop is irrelevant, for these horses are not required to go across country at speed.

A sloping riding shoulder is neither necessary nor desirable in a harness horse. Such a shoulder will not carry a collar in a suitable position for effective traction without causing discomfort to the horse. R. H. Smythe, a noted British veterinary surgeon and author of many books on the horse, gives the following desirable measurements for a good, laid-back riding shoulder. 'It shoud have', he wrote 'a degree of inclination, measured from the point of the shoulder to the junction of neck and withers, of approximately 60 degrees. From the point of the shoulder to the centre of the withers, their highest point, should give a reading of 43 degrees. From the point of the shoulder to the junction of the withers and back, the reading should be 40 degrees'. Excellent advice for English hunters, but not much good for Andalucians, Lipizzaners, Saddlers and so on.

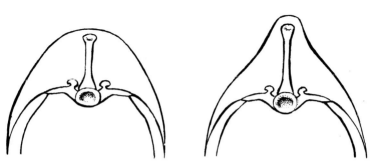

Fig. 6 (left) Flat withers with loaded shoulders. (right) Well-formed withers.

All horses, however, need to have straight, muscular forelegs without the limb being 'tied-in' at the elbow. The forelegs must be free from the body to operate effectively. Essentials for the foreleg are a long, very muscular forearm; a flat, big, low-set knee; a flat, not a round or fleshy, fetlock joint, and pasterns which have no exaggerated slope, either towards being upright or the converse. If the knee is high off the ground it follows that the cannon will also be long and thus less strong and less able to carry weight. Big, flat knees with prominent pisiform bones allow ample room for the flexor tendons to pass downwards.

The pastern, which forms the shock absorber of the body mass, will give a most comfortable, springy ride if it is long and sloped, but this conformation is not desirable since long, sloped pasterns place great strain on the suspensory ligament and the tendons running down the rear of the leg. Upright pasterns are just as unfortunate since they cannot fulfil their function of absorbing concussion sufficiently and can therefore cause unsoundness in the leg. Hind pasterns, which fill the same role, are always a little shorter than those on the forelegs because the hocks have a compensating flexing action.

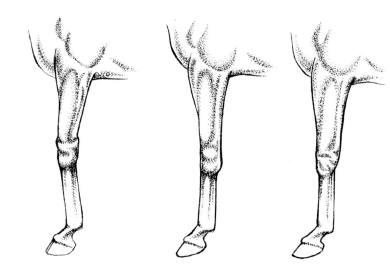

Fig. 7 Faults of the forelegs. (left) Over at the knee. (centre) Back of the knee. (right) Tied in below the knee (= light of bone).

Poor forelegs are those which are 'tied-in below the knee', 'back of the knee' or which are 'light of bone'. 'Tied-in below the knee' means the measurement round the leg, immediately below the knee, is less than that taken lower down the leg above the fetlock joint. This is a serious weakness and predisposes the horse to almost certain unsoundness. 'Back of the knee' means the leg curves inwards below the knee. It is another weakness to be avoided.

'Too light of bone' poses the question 'how light?' In general terms the ability of the horse to carry weight (his own and that of a rider) is governed largely by the *strength* or quality of bone below the knee. A measurement of 20 cm is considered about right for a hunter of 16 hh, and anything below that will not be considered satisfactory. A blood-type of pony, like quality British show ponies, will probably need not more than 16·5 cm, whereas a cart-horse might have 25–28 cm of bone. Frankly, 'bone' is in danger of becoming a part of the horse 'mystique', and much nonsense is talked about it. The quantity of bone is not as important as the quality. It is thought that the bone of Thoroughbreds and Arabs is of greater density than that of the 'commoners' and will, therefore, inch for inch, carry more weight. All bone is tubular and has a hollow centre filled with marrow. Obviously strength depends on the thickness and density of bone surrounding the central core, the smaller the core the greater being the overall strength of the tube. Common bone is said to be coarser in structure and with a larger central core. There is, however, no way of evaluating bone in the live animal other than by measurement — a process which clearly is open to error.

At the bottom of the foreleg and the hindleg, too, is the foot, and here the horsey adage 'no foot — no 'oss' is entirely true. In the cold-blood breeds the feet are obviously larger and more plate-like, the better to cope with work on soft, wet agricultural land, but whatever the breed or type of horse some general rules apply. In the first place a foot must be equal in size and shape to its partner – uneven feet with one smaller than another, for instance, reveal that the smaller one has some record of unsoundness. Horses naturally relieve pain in a foot by standing on the other, sound one. As a result the unsound foot will tend to shrink because it is not carrying its proper weight. Secondly, a foot with a dropped sole is likely to cause trouble. The sole should be slightly concave in the fore-foot and more so in the hind, and it should not give to pressure from the fingers. In order for the frog, the anti-concussion and anti-slip device, to be well-formed and in contact with the ground the heels of the foot must be open and in no way contracted. 'Boxy', donkey feet, where the frog is shrivelled because no ground contact is possible, are a disadvantage, as are brittle hooves showing signs of breakage and longitudinal cracking. White-walled hooves, usually found with white lower limbs, are of softer horn than the dark, blue-grey walls and are thought to be more prone to wear.

Feet should point straight to the front. Turned out feet predispose to serious brushing; pigeon-toes, on the other hand, usually indicate a defective 'dishing' action (that is, one where the leg is carried outwards in circular fashion). The correct angle of slope for the foot of a riding horse is about 50 degrees for the forefeet and between 55 and 60 degrees for the hindfeet. These opinions of ideal horse feet are expressed from a northern European standpoint, and perhaps particularly from a British one. They would not necessarily find acceptance in Spain and Portugal, where horses have very boxy feet, as is often the case in hot climates, and where farriery is primitive. However it is only fair to say that the horses manage well. The shoeing of American show horses, like the Saddlers, is just as unacceptable to European eyes, however skilful it may be. But again the enormously long feet and heavy shoes are for a particular purpose and these practices should not be judged by the criteria of the British hunting field.

The first part of the trunk to consider is the chest, which one notable authority insisted could not be too wide. This is the sort of sweeping generalization which becomes well-known and is quite wrong. The chest can be too wide, particularly in a riding horse, when it will cause an objectionable rolling action. The chest must have sufficient width, for its size and shape controls the degree of expansion of the lungs. The shape of the chest is dependent upon the curvature of the ribs. If they are well-sprung the chest must be correspondingly generous. Flat-sided horses have narrow chests

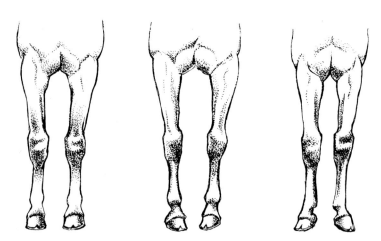

Fig. 8 Influence of chest width on forelegs: (left) Chest not too narrow or too wide; legs straight, feet straight ahead. (centre) 'Bosomy', over-wide chest; 'pigeon toes'. (right) Chest too narrow; legs look as if they are 'coming out of one hole'; feet turned out.

which naturally cause the forelegs to be set too close – a deficiency graphically described by the term 'both legs out of the same hole'. When the forelegs are set too close the danger of brushing will obviously be increased.

The girth, or barrel, of the horse needs to be deep to contain the internal organs and a competition horse measuring less than 1·8 m round the girth could not be considered. Well-sprung ribs are particularly important and they should give the appearance of going well back into the loins. Horses that look as though they need another rib between the last rib and the quarters ('short of a rib') are seriously at fault. They will rarely have reserves of stamina and will run up very light in work, the junction between trunk and quarters much resembling that of a greyhound.

Obviously, the back of the horse is the weakest part of a structure that is not, if we are honest, best suited to the carrying of weight. It must, therefore, irrespective of the purpose to which the horse is put, be as strong as possible. Any weakness in the back will show up in the performance. Clearly the two extremities of the back, the withers in front and the loins and quarters behind, must be equally well-made. In a saddle horse the back must be shaped so as to be able to carry a saddle well. If there is no place for a saddle the horse is useless – at least for riding. The back should be considered before the rest of the frame. Pony judges, as well as some judges of Arabs, who pay a lot of attention to the beauty of the head and almost exclude the rest of the animal, would do well to remember the outspoken comment of a noted Welsh judge who was fond of reminding his audiences that 'you don't ride on his bloody 'ead!'

Roach backs, or their opposite, the pronounced hollow backs are rarely worth considering; the former being particularly associated with faulty action and an uncomfortable ride. Both varieties increase the difficulties of saddle fitting. Very long backs are an obvious weakness, while very short ones, though strong, restrict the movement of the quarters and are never associated with speed. Also an over-short back can be uncomfortable for the rider, who cannot avoid receiving the full propulsive thrust of the hindlegs. Such spinal flexion of which the horse is capable will also be seriously reduced. (Spinal flexion can only take place between the last of the dorsal vertebrae and the first of the lumbar.)

The area between the last rib and the croup of the horse is the loin and, as the link between the quarters and the trunk, it must be strong and muscular. The croup, the highest point behind the saddle, will be above the level of the withers in the young horse, but should be level with the withers when the horse reaches maturity. A mature horse with a croup higher than his withers will be driven on to his forehand and it will be difficult, if not impossible, to effect a re-balancing. Such a croup should not, however, be confused with a 'goose rump', a high, well-muscled croup often associated with jumpers and with horses of 'common' parentage. Often in such cases the tail will be set a little lower than is strictly desirable for good quarters. Arab horses, or those strongly indebted to that most ancient of the horse breeds, will have a straight croup, accompanied by a characteristic high tail position – the pure-bred Arab 'bannering' his tail to the point of carrying it almost vertical when in movement. The Arab conformation here, as elsewhere, differs from other breeds because of the Arab's unique structure: the Arabian horse has nineteen ribs, instead of the usual eighteen, and five lumbar bones instead of six.

The best position from which to assess the quarters is directly from behind. This is where the power comes from and should give an impression of strength, the well-rounded quarters filling out until the gaskins (or second thighs) appear to be the widest point. The shape of the gaskins and the relative position of the hock reveals a propensity for speed or otherwise. In the saddle horse, where speed is mostly a matter of some importance, the ideal second thigh will be long and muscular and will, therefore, be accompanied with hocks set comparatively low to the ground. Draught horses, on the other hand, will usually have a much shorter (and possibly) stronger second thigh with a correspondingly high hock joint and long hind cannon. Lack of muscular development between the thighs, termed

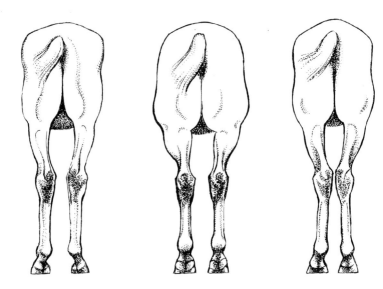

Fig. 9 Influence of quarters on hindlegs: (left) Weak quarters 'split up behind' (thighs dividing just under dock); hindlegs too close. (centre) Strong quarters with good, well-developed second thigh. (right) Weak quarters and 'cow hocks' (inward turning).

Fig. 10 (centre) Ideal position for the hock is when a vertical line can connect the buttock and point of hock, to continue down the back of the cannon. Hocks to the rear or front of this line are less good for speed; however the hock and cannon are often carried in front of the vertical in hunters and jumpers, giving thrust for jumping.

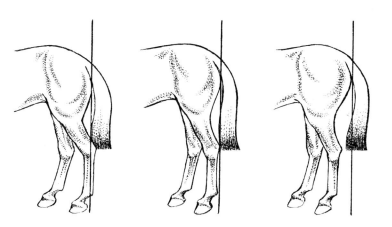

'split up behind', indicates a lack of strength in an essential department. Heavy thighs which join low down and force the animal to move wide behind in the classic 'wet-knicker trot' are nearly as objectionable.

The main points to look for in the quarters are in the hock and its position and shape. The ideal hock for the riding horse has its point set on a line with the chestnut (a scaly oval protuberance lying above the knee on the foreleg). This represents true proportion and gives maximum efficiency. As before, the hock on the riding horse is preferably set low to the ground. The ideal position of the hock in relation to the buttocks and cannon for speed is in a position where a straight line can be drawn from buttock to point of hock and can be continued down the back of the cannon. Hocks which are positioned to the rear of this imaginary line indicate an obvious lack of propulsive power. When the joints are carried to the front of the line, and are overstraight, a similar loss of power will result and in both instances the hocks will be susceptible to damage when subjected to work. Frequently, however, in hunters and jumpers, as well as in draught horses, the hocks and cannons are held in front of the vertical. This position does not improve speed, but it does give strength and supplies thrust for jumping.

'Bad hocks' are those in which the joint is forced to accept a greater than desirable strain and may as a result be more prone to disease and injury. In this category are sickle hocks, which are too much overbent or curved on the *front* edge; 'bow' hocks, where the joints are turned out; and 'cow' hocks, where they are turned inwards. Most authorities condemn all three, the only exceptions being those whose breeds exhibit one or other of these faults.

It is obvious that the action of any horse should, for reasons of mechanical efficiency, be straight and true. Toes should not turn in or out; hindfeet should 'track up', that is the hindfoot landing in front of the imprint made by the forefoot; 'dishing' and 'plaiting', the crossing of the forelegs when in motion, inhibit a true and economical action and are also dangerous. Such faults would be frowned upon in an English or American show ring, where horses are judged for their riding suitability. However, in the Andalucian a high, uneconomic action, with forelegs waving like windmills, is much prized as part of the breed character. This is also true of horses in some of the American classes. One authority on the Morgan horse, a very versatile American breed, wrote recently that the action of the Morgan park horse is 'basically, a simple circular, wheel-like action with a deal of shoulder movement'. Such action could hardly fail to cause some loss of forward progression.

Thus, international views on conformation and its corollary, action, are neither entirely consistent nor always logical. It is possible to lay down practical general standards for riding horses, draught horses etc., but there will always be exceptions, governed by human whims rather than mechanical efficiency. Desirable conformation and action are judged according to the purpose for which the horse is required, and the best conformation for a purpose is assessed differently in different countries.

In Britain horse judging at shows is carried out by one, or sometimes two, experienced officials invited by the show committee.

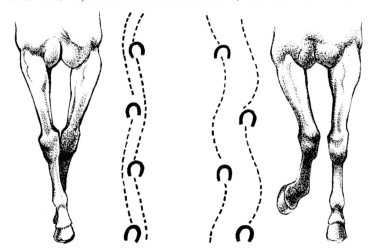

Fig. 11 Faults in foreleg action: (left) Plaiting. (right) Dishing.

Judges are not professionals and qualify for their position because of their experience and by the acceptance of their peers. Exhibitors, by bringing their horses before a judge in a show class, are inviting the judge to express an opinion on their horses. In the British show ring that is what judging is all about and it is a matter of opinion expressed by the judge in the placings of the class. Horses are, or should be, judged on their performance on the day, without reference to previous form.

British judges watch their class at walk, trot, canter and, where appropriate, the gallop. They subject the entries to a searching individual examination and then, in ridden classes, will ride the exhibits to confirm any impressions already made. Much store is placed on the ride that a horse gives to a judge and it reveals much about the animal's training and temperament. A great deal depends upon the integrity and skill of the judges, whose influence upon horse and pony breeding is considerable. On the whole it works very well indeed.

Elsewhere the system is different. In the United States of America the element of personal opinion is eliminated, as far as possible, by the insistence on detailed breed or type standards and by the frequent employment of a panel of judges. Additionally, and most importantly, actual performance in the ring is the criterion and is judged on a comprehensive marking system. Hunters and ponies in Britain are judged, outside what are known as 'working' classes where the performance element predominates, without the entries being jumped. Show hunter and show pony classes are therefore essentially 'beauty competitions', held for the purpose of finding the model of near perfection. It is presumed that if a hunter is of good conformation, has presence, manners and can also gallop, then jumping is only a matter of training. In any case, many people believe that the fences erected in a show ring bear little relation to those met in the hunting field.

Recently the Swedish system of judging has become popular in Europe. This system involves a panel of judges independently awarding marks out of five or ten for each particular part of the body, for instance the head and neck, shoulders and forelegs, back etc. Each individual judge's marks for each part are then added together and averaged. In theory the North American system, despite its undoubted artificiality, and even more the Swedish system, should give the fairest and most nearly correct result. However in practice this is not always the case for horses do not lend themselves to being judged by committee. In some European countries where horse-breeding has become the concern of the state rather than of the individual, and also in the USSR, horses are judged by a performance test. Each animal is subjected to specific speed, jumping and stamina tests at a certain age. The method is pragmatic but the wastage rate can be high, many horses being insufficiently developed for tests of the severity imposed.

Glossary

Action — the movement of a horse's legs.

Back of the knee — conformational fault in which the forelegs are curved backwards.

Bone — strength and length of bone below a horse's knee, determining the horse's ability to carry weight.

Bosomy — describes an over-wide chest.

Both legs out of the same hole — appearance of front legs resulting from too narrow chest.

Bow hocks — outward-turned hock joints; a conformational fault.

Boxy feet — hooves 'boxed in' like a donkey's, preventing the FROG from reaching the ground.

Breed — equine group whose members have been selectively bred for consistent characteristics, with pedigrees recorded in a Stud Book. cf TYPE.

Brushing — hoof or shoe striking the inside of opposite leg at or near fetlock; usually caused by poor conformation or action.

Cold-blood — generic name for the heavy European horse breeds descended from the prehistoric Forest horse. cf WARM-BLOOD.

Colt — uncastrated male horse less than 4 years old.

Common, common-bred — any horse not of pure or near-pure blood.

Common bone — BONE of inferior quality, coarse-grained, lacking density, with a large central core.

Conformation — the way in which a horse is 'put together', with particular regard to its proportions.

Cow hocks — hocks which turn inwards in the manner of a cow; the opposite conformational fault to BOW HOCKS.

Donkey feet — *see* BOXY FEET.

Dished profile — concave head profile, typical of Arabian horse.

Dishing — faulty ACTION in which lower legs describe a 'dish-shaped' outward movement.

Ewe neck — Faulty neck conformation: a concave curve of the back of the neck.

Filly	female horse under 4 years old.
Forehand	part of horse in front of rider: head, neck, shoulders, withers and forelegs.
Frog	rubbery, triangular pad of horn between the bars under the hoof; it acts as a shock-absorber.
Gaskin	second thigh.
Gelding	castrated male horse.
Hand	unit of measurement of horse's height. One hand = approx 10cm (4in)
Heavy horse	any large draught horse, e.g. Suffolk Punch, Percheron, etc.
Hindquarters	the part of a horse's body from the rear of the flank to the beginning of the tail, and downwards to the top of the second thigh.
Hollow back	concave, sagging back in the area of the loins; the opposite conformational fault to a ROACH BACK.
Light horse	any horse suitable for riding, except a Thoroughbred.
Light of bone	BONE of insufficient density, cf COMMON BONE.
Make and shape	horse-lover's parlance for CONFORMATION.
Mare	female horse 4 or more years old.
Outcross	adaptation of a breed by crossing it with another breed.
Pedigree	ancestry of a quality horse, as recorded in a Stud Book.
Pigeon toes	conformational fault in which the feet point inwards.
Plaiting	faulty ACTION in which the feet are placed in front of each other.
Points	external features of a horse, comprising its CONFORMATION.
Quality	refinement in breeding and conformation, lending a breed its distinctive appearance.
Quarters	*see* HINDQUARTERS.
Roach back	convex curvature of the spine in the loin area; the opposite conformational fault to a HOLLOW BACK.

Roman profile   convex head profile usually associated with common stock (the Andalucian is an exception).

Short of a rib   conformational fault of slack loins, caused by too wide a space between the point of the hip and the last rib.

Sickle hocks   conformational fault: seen from the side, the hocks are too strongly angled at the joint, causing weakness of the hindlegs.

Split up behind   conformational fault caused by weakness of the second thighs; seen from behind, the thighs divide too high, just beneath the dock.

Stallion   uncastrated male horse 4 or more years old.

Stud Book   Book kept by a breed society in which the pedigrees of pure-bred stock are recorded.

Substance   the physical quality of a horse's body, in terms of musculature, tendons, etc.

Swan neck   conformational fault in which the upper neck curves upwards so that the head joins it in a nearly vertical line.

Tied in below the knee   legs that are much narrower just below the knee than further down towards the fetlock joint; a conformational fault indicating that a horse is LIGHT OF BONE.

Type   Horses which fulfil a particular purpose (e.g. cob, hunter, hack) but do not belong to a specific breed.

Warm-blood   generic term applied to any fine-framed breed or type of LIGHT HORSE suitable for riding, and assumed to descend from the prehistoric Plateau horse via the Tarpan. of COLD-BLOOD.

Bibliography

Archer, R., Pearson, C. and Covey, C. *The Crabbet Arabian Stud*. Alexander Heriot, 1978.

Chivers, K. *The Shire Horse: A History of the Breed and the Men*. J. A. Allen, 1976.

Dent, A. *The Horse Through Fifty Centuries of Civilization*. Phaidon, 1974.

Dossenbach, M. and H. D. *Great Stud Farms of the World*. Thames and Hudson, 1978.

Goodad, D. M. *Horses of the World*. David and Charles, 1973.

Goodad, D. M. *Horses and Their World*. David and Charles, 1976.

Glyn, R. *The World's Finest Horses and Ponies*. Harrap, 1971.

Greely, M. *Arabian Exodus*. J. A. Allen, 1975.

Hartley Edwards, E. (ed.). *Encyclopedia of the Horse*. Octopus, 1977.

Hartley Edwards, E. *From Paddock to Saddle*. Pelham Books, 1972.

Hartley Edwards, E. *The Horseman's Guide*. Country Life, 1969.

Summerhays, R. S. *Encyclopedia for Horsemen*. Frederick Warne, 1975 (revised ed.).

Trench, C. C. *A History of Horsemanship*. Longman, 1970.

Williams, D. *Great Riding Schools of the World*. Weidenfeld and Nicholson, 1975.

Acknowledgements

Photographs

Diederick d'Ailly, CBC, Toronto 189 top; Animal Photography, London – Gunnar Dahl 125 bottom; Animal Photography – Georg G. Harrap 187 top; Animal Photography – Zofia Raczkowska 101 top; Animal Photography – Dr Stain 131 bottom; Animal Photography – Sally Anne Thompson 17 bottom, 19 top, 20, 21 top, 21 bottom, 22, 23 top, 23 bottom, 25 top, 27 top, 27 bottom, 29, 30–31, 32–33, 33 top, 35 top, 37 top, 39 top, 39 bottom, 40, 41 top, 41 bottom, 42, 43 top, 43 bottom, 45 top, 45 bottom, 47 top, 47 bottom, 49 top, 49 bottom, 53 top, 57 top, 57 bottom, 65 top, 65 bottom, 67 top, 67 bottom, 69 bottom, 73 top, 73 bottom, 75 bottom, 77 bottom, 81 top, 81 bottom, 83 top, 83 bottom, 85 bottom, 87 bottom, 91 top, 93 top, 93 bottom, 95 top, 95 bottom, 97 top, 101 bottom, 103 top, 103 bottom, 105 bottom, 107 top, 107 bottom, 109 bottom, 111 bottom, 121 top, 121 bottom, 125 top, 127 top, 129 top, 133 top right, 133 bottom, 135 top, 137 top, 137 bottom, 141 top, 145 bottom, 147 top, 147 bottom, 149 top, 149 bottom, 151 top, 153 bottom, 173 bottom, 179 top, 179 bottom, 187 bottom, 191 bottom, 193 top, 193 bottom, 195 bottom, 203 bottom; Ardea, London 157 top; Ardea – Jean-Paul Ferrero 17 top; Ardea – Pat Morris 99 bottom; Judith Campbell, Hythe – G. Argent 173 top, 177 bottom; Judith Campbell – N. Toyne 200 bottom; Bruce Coleman, Uxbridge 199 bottom; Bruce Coleman – Jane Burton 157 bottom; Bruce Coleman – Hans Reinhard 79 bottom, 87 top; Werner Ernst, Warendorf 71 top, 75 top; Jean-Paul Ferrero, Grigny 59 top; Robert Harding Associates, London 209 top; Robert Harding Associates – Garner 182–183; Robert Harding Associates – Ian Summer 185 bottom; P. Russell Howell, Kingsettle Stud, Salisbury 201 top; Jacana, Paris 51 top, 55 bottom; Jacana – G. Trouillet 63 bottom; Fylkesagronen Gunnar Kvaerner, Kløfta 123 bottom; Leslie Lane, Burgess Hill 18–19; Joja Lewenhaupt, Tjörnarp 129 bottom, 131 top; Jane Miller, London 185 top; Pony of the Americas, Mason City, Iowa 203 top; Popperfoto, London 171 bottom; Mrs D. Rivaz, British Appaloosa Society, Tylers Causeway 195 top; Spectrum, London 24–25, 53 bottom; Tony Stone Associates, London 31 top, 35 bottom, 36–37, 61 bottom; Elizabeth Weiland, Zollikon 69 top, 123 top; Dr Norbert Zalis 88–89, 89 top.

Index

Page numbers in **bold** type refer to main descriptions and facing illustrations.